INDEX
ON CENSORSHIP

INDEX ON CENSORSHIP 2 2000

INDEX

Volume 29 No 2 March/April 2000 Issue 193

WEBSITE NEWS UPDATED WEEKLY

www.indexoncensorship.org
contact@indexoncensorship.org
tel: 020 7278 2313
fax: 020 7278 1878

Index on Censorship (ISSN 0306-4220) is published bi-monthly by a non-profit-making company: Writers & Scholars International Ltd, Lancaster House, 33 Islington High Street, London N1 9LH. *Index on Censorship* is associated with Writers & Scholars Educational Trust, registered charity number 325003
Periodicals postage: (US subscribers only) paid at Newark, New Jersey. Postmaster: send US address changes to *Index on Censorship* c/o Mercury Airfreight International Ltd Inc, 365 Blair Road, Avenel, NJ 07001, USA
© This selection Writers & Scholars International Ltd, London 1999
© Contributors to this issue, except where otherwise indicated

Subscriptions (6 issues per annum)
Individuals: UK £39, US $52, rest of world £45
Institutions: UK £44, US $80, rest of world £50
Speak to Tony Callaghan on 020 7278 2313

EDITORIAL

Private places

Despite women's collective achievements over the past century, there have always been profound divisions between them, and none greater than in attitudes to pornography. *Index* confronts the women in the US and the UK who want to ban pornography, arguing that they misrepresent both its content and its effects, as well as misunderstanding the culture in which we live and the 'peculiar nature of fantasy' (p45).

There are other issues where women censor and silence – both themselves and others. It is, for instance, mainly women who insist on clitorodectomies for their daughters (p73). Women in Zimbabwe remain silent, and risk further infection, rather than admit to family members dying of AIDS (p172). Asian mothers and mothers-in-law may kill their young women, saying they act 'not out of choice but responsibility'(p82), while in eastern Europe (p76) there is overwhelming silence from the victims of violence in that sacrosanct private place – the home.

And this, of course, is the nub of the argument: women are the guardians of that private place and if they censor, however monstrously, they say they do it to protect themselves, their daughters, their culture. Yet, ironically, it is often the misogyny embedded in the cultures they are protecting – whether western or eastern – that makes life so precarious for them.

At a time when all Europe is watching Jörg Haider's Freedom Party in Austria, our file on that other Europe further east reports on disturbing levels of racism in countries that will be future partners in an expanded EU. Rafal Pankowski deplores the fact that the far right has entered the heart of Polish mainstream politics (p143), while Anatolii Pristavkin sees that the promotion of Nazism and racism attracts no opprobrium in his native Russia (p136). Is collective envy at the root of all this, asks the Hungarian writer George Konrad (p149)? Certainly on this subject, as Ludvik Vaculik suggests in his sharply satirical piece (p132), we need look no further than into our own hearts: the implicit racism in the British Home Secretary's recent remark, taken up with alacrity by some of the media, that he wanted to see *all* the people on the hijacked Afghan jet removed from Britain 'as soon as reasonably practicable' made nonsense of his quasi-judicial role in deciding their fate. Meanwhile, as David Irving's libel case against Deborah Lipstadt puts historical truth on trial in the place least appropriate to judge it, a court, we publish Norman Finkelstein's essay (p120) on the Holocaust industry and the influence of Holocaust denial in the USA. ❏

contents

Women who censor: When sex
rears its head,
universal sisterhood
flies out of the window

p34

Austria is not the only European
country where racism and
xenophobia are at the heart of
government.

p130

Raking over the ashes:
Finkelstein on the Holocaust industry p120

CONTENTS

5   EDITORIAL Ursula Owen

8   IN THE NEWS

         NEWS ANALYSIS
4   UK Tony Geraghty Tapping into the future
8   ISRAEL Neil Sammonds Israel in a spin
2   RUSSIA Dmitry Bykov Between a rock and a hard place
6   SOUTH AFRICA Njabulo Ndebele The race card

2   LEGAL Helene Guldberg The perils of nuance

4   WOMEN WHO CENSOR
6   Elizabeth Wilson Women who censor
5   Lynne Segal Pornographic battles
3   Judith Levine The dumb-luck club
8   STATISTICS Defining porn
0   Maryam Azad Sisters of darkness
6   Shadafarin Ghadirian Suspended in time
3   STATISTICS Female genital mutilation
6   Irena Maryniak Something to think about
2   Yasmin Alibhai-Brown Smother love
5   Jasmina Tesanovic Mothers and daughters
8   Gordana Igric Censor with a flower

0   FLASHPOINTS Man in the balance
2   INDEX INDEX

0   OPINION Norman Finkelstein The Holocaust industry

0   EASTERN EUROPE: RACISM ACROSS BORDERS
2   CZECH REPUBLIC Ludvik Vaculik I don't like the look of you, stranger!
6   RUSSIA Anatolii Pristavkin Not one of us
3   POLAND Rafal Pankowski Met any Jews lately?
9   HUNGARY George Konrad The pitfalls of community

         CULTURE
6   BURKINA FASO Michael Kelly Stories of an African schoolgirl
9   BURKINA FASO Dienobou Sanoussa Circle of fire/A crime
4   UK Michael Griffin Positive negatives
1   USA ACLU Squaring the circle

2   BABEL Kim Normanton The silence of the damned
9   NEW MEDIA Danny Schechter Old commies v dot.comies
4   LETTER Salil Tripathi Soccer moms put in the boot
0   DIARY Neil Sammonds An image of flowers

in the news

● **Scent off** China withdrew commercial registration for Yves Saint-Laurent's 'Opium' perfume in late December, effectively banning it from sale. It was the aggressive selling of opium by foreign merchants in the 19th century that precipitated China's fall from empire to impoverished colony within decades. 'Poison' and 'Obsession' are still on the shelves.

● **Panic stations** Video artist Mike Zieper and his web host, Mark Wieger, are taking the FBI to court for violating their freedom of speech. Zieper's alleged crime was to put online *Military Takeover*, a film which dramatised public fears about Y2K disasters in the form of a news broadcast. FBI agents immediately contacted Wieger and told him to remove it, claiming it raised security concerns. The ACLU says that the government agents thereby suppressed 'constitutionally protected speech and due process rights when they sought to censor the film'.

● **Candour standards** East Timor decided in February to adopt Portuguese as its official language, against the wishes of the 90% of its people who speak only the local Tetun, or the Bahasa Indonesian which was imposed during 24 years of military occupation. Most Portuguese-speakers were educated during the colonial era, leading to accusations of elitism from younger activists. In newly democratised Indonesia, meanwhile, journalists are striving to purge Bahasa of the detritus of euphemisms and military jargon instilled over three decades of authoritarian rule with a view to setting 'new standards for candour'. First for the chop are the terms 'pre-prosperity' for poverty, 'procedural error' for official corruption and 'rogue individual' for a member of a military death squad.

● **Baby with the Ba'ath** In mid-January President Saddam Hussein ordered the banning of satirical comments and cartoons which criticise the 'performance of government and its institutions'. Journalists were told that 'saying things were so funny, you have to laugh' no longer 'befits the accomplishments' of the ruling Ba'athist party, 'nor the difficult circumstances imposed on Iraq'. Writers of satirical columns in seven newspapers were either banned or asked to change their style.

● **Haider hangover** Critics of Jörg Haider, leader of the far-right Freedom Party which convulsed European opinion when it formed a coalition with the ailing People's Party on 8 February, are now getting their come-uppance. Columnist Gerhard Marschall of the *Oberös/tereichische Nachtrichren* was fired when he refused an order to tone down his criticism of Haider, because 'it was losing the paper subscribers'. And Austria's most popular comic duo, Christopher Grissemann and Dirk Stermann, face a Freedom Party lawsuit for telling an interviewer: 'Somebody should shoot Haider. Someone who has only two months left to live.'

● **Ethical airbrush** CBS anchorman Dan Rather, a voice of probity in an otherwise probationary century, cried foul when his network indulged in a little reality-tweaking during the New Year's Eve celebrations. The company has technology which can superimpose a digitally created CBS logo on anything from a passing car to the side of the General Motors building. It used it to cover up a neon sign sponsored by rival network NBC during Dan's traditional end-of-year show in Times Square. 'There is no excuse for it,' said a remorseful Rather. 'I did not grasp the ethical implications of this, and that was wrong on my part.'

● **Bad taste award** A Taiwan restaurant decorated with photographs of Nazi concentration camp victims was forced to redecorate in January after a complaint by Israel's diplomatic representative to Taipei, Uri Gutman. 'The Jail' opened last December, decorated with watch towers and a wall-painting of inmates behind barbed wire. A sign reading 'gas chambers' indicated the entrance to the toilets, which were suitably done out with open pipes and valves. 'We did this very innocently,' said proprietor Stone Cheng, 'these things are very far away from us.'

● **Didgerydoodoo** Australian art lovers have been spared the avant-garde pleasures of Chris Ofili's faeces-splattered *Virgin Mary*. The painting is part of a peripatetic exhibition, *Sensation*, which was unsuccessfully banned in 1999 by New York mayor Rudy Giuliani (*Index* 1/2000). The National Gallery of Australia was due to host the collection in June 2000, but gallery director Brian Kennedy cancelled, allegedly bowing to pressure from Arts Minister Richard Alston. Alston is fast developing a reputation as the censors' censor: he is the prime mover behind Australia's new Internet censorship regime (*Index* 4/1999).

● **They don't give a dam** ITV kick-started the UK's pre-Christmas season with *The DamBusters* – a recreation of the RAF's 'bouncing bombs' raid on German dams in WWII. The 1950s movie sticks closely to the facts right down to the name of Wing Commander Guy Gibson's Labrador, Nigger. Mown down by a jeep halfway through, his name becomes the codeword for the bombers' prime target. Yet the word 'nigger' was completely excised from the ITV edit. The dog's every appearance is greeted by oddly clipped conversation and, as the dam heads skywards, an apparently silent radio message generates headquarters' jubilation. ITV laid the blame on London Weekend Television (LWT), but LWT spokesman Rowan O'Sullivan strongly denied an official censorship policy, claiming that the 'politically correct' version shown to millions had been edited by a junior member of staff without higher approval.

● **That's all, Folks!** Beijing has snatched Elmer Fudd's blunderbuss and blown away Bugs for ever. The Cartoon Network, a cable channel belonging to Ted Turner's media empire, was ordered to stop transmitting Bugs Bunny to its 100,000 subscribers in January. 'They know perfectly well what they've done wrong.' chided an official, without saying quite what the network had done wrong. A spokesman for the network was baffled by the possibilities for subversion inherent in the rabbit's adventures. However, amid a ratings war for the attention of Chinese youth, it has been suggested that the government hopes to develop home-grown cartoon 'products', imbued with patriotism, public spirit and planned socialist humour.

● **Secret map of censorship**
On 22 January two women poets and a publisher were sent to prison for two months for writings that the court said 'included expressions that violate God, and indecent and shameless expressions'.

Dr 'Aliya Shu'ayb, professor of philosophy at Kuwait University, was found guilty of blasphemy and of 'publishing opinions that ridicule religion' in *Spiders Bemoan a Wound*, a book of poetry published in 1993. Shu'ayb and publisher Yahia al-Rubay'an were also fined 100 dinars (US$328) for distributing the work without a permit. Shu'ayb's lawyer has said that the only part of the book that mentions God at all is the phrase 'God's secret map'. Shu'ayb has said she will appeal against the conviction.

Poet Leila al-'Othman was similarly convicted of using indecent language in her book *The Departure*, which had been approved by government censors in 1984. Al-'Othman's lawyers said that words such as 'lustful' were used in describing the relationship of one sea wave with another, but that it did not have a sexual connotation; and that one desperate character tells his roommates that they can rape him, but this merely represented his psychological state. Al-'Othman said that she had obtained affadavits from professors of Islamic law attesting that her poem did not touch on religion. The court ignored them.

Kuwait's Press and Publications Law makes it a criminal offence to publish materials that violate 'by allusion, slander, sarcasm or disparagement, God or the prophets or the companions of the Prophet Mohammad, or sully public morals'. An equally vague article in the criminal code mandates prison sentences for identical offences, although the judges in these two cases did not specify what they found offensive in the books. Or, indeed, need to.

Index correspondent

● **Define 'apparatus'** Does the jurisdiction of the official film censor in Ireland extend to television broadcasting? That's a question set to be answered in the courts, following intervention by the Department of Justice to prevent the film *Natural Born Killers* being screened by the independent commercial station TV3. The department argues that the film had already been banned from Irish cinemas by film censor Sheamus Smith.

An edited version of the film was scheduled for late-night, weekend screening by TV3 on 30 January, with advance warnings that it was suitable only for adults. The schedule had been approved in advance by the Independent Radio and Television Commission, the statutory body for broadcasting. But it was withdrawn following late intervention by the Department of Justice, which warned that it would otherwise seek a court order to prevent it being shown. The station screened an alternative, with on-screen messages to explain why *Natural Born Killers* had been shelved.

A Department of Justice spokesman played down the intervention but TV3 boss Rick Hetherington called it 'ridiculous', pointing out that the department had invoked legislation dating back to 1923 to stop the screening. 'We are also considering our legal options,' he said, 'and intend to seek a judicial review to clarify the position. This is an important issue, with major implications for all TV services operating here, including Pay TV and the cable companies.'

In its letter to TV3, the Department of Justice had cited Section 5 of the Censorship of Films Act of 1923, which says: 'No film shall be exhibited in public by means of a cinematograph, or similar apparatus, unless and until the official censor has certified that the whole of such picture is fit for exhibition in public.'

Anthony Garvey

● **To lose two is downright careless** In what some analysts regard as the most significant defection since the flight of the Dalai Lama in 1959, the 17th Karmapa Lama, 14-year-old Ugyen Trinley Dorje, left his monastery near Lhasa on 28 December and arrived in Dharamsala, northern India, having crossed 900 miles of the Himalayas with a small entourage. His defection was

particularly embarrassing for the Chinese government which had agreed with, and endorsed, the Dalai Lama's 1992 recognition of the boy as the Karmapa Lama, leader of one of the four major sects of Tibetan Buddhism.

Beijing was grooming the boy to present him as an alternative leader to the 'splittist' Dalai Lama. But he, it appears, finally lost patience with being refused permission to visit his spiritual teachers in Sikkim. In a gesture suggesting he would be shown lenience should he return, *Xinhua* reported the boy's disappearance, but only that he had left to collect 'ceremonial artefacts'. Beijing quickly made it clear to New Delhi that, for the sake of preserving relations, political asylum should not be offered. New Delhi has yet to make a firm decision on the boy's status.

During his first audience on 4 February, the Karmapa Lama said that to practise Buddhism, 'one has to be free' and that he hoped 'all the people of Tibet will soon be able to win their freedom'. Unwelcome words to a red-faced Beijing struggling to make sense of its current Tibet policy.

Meanwhile, on 16 January, the Chinese authorities nominated a two-year-old Tibetan child, Soinam Puncog, as the seventh Reting Lama, announcing the child would be brought up to 'love Communism and respect the integrity of the motherland'. The Dalai Lama's office was quick to reject the nomination, saying the Reting's soul 'has not yet been reborn'. Beijing now claims a shaky authority over three of Tibetan Buddhism's highest figures – the Reting, Panchen and Karmapa lamas. The Reting Lama is particularly significant since he would be regent upon the Dalai Lama's death and therefore instrumental in recognising his reincarnation.

Index correspondent

● **Mitch and the coyote**
Reports that up to 5,000 natives of the Mosquitia are on the verge of starvation due to poor food production after Hurricane Mitch, which appeared in the dailies *La Tribuna* and *El Heraldo* last December, have been rejected by indigenous leaders. According to Edgardo Benitez, Tawahka leader and environmentalist, the claims are no more than a ploy cooked up by US citizen Thomas Harner in order to obtain donations from aid agencies to trade for gold panned in the area.

Benitez and other Tawahka said that Harner's allies are Luis Martinez, a teacher from Tukrum, and Paulino Ordonez from Yapuwas, both of whom have made statements to the press. But they have never worked or co-operated with any community organisation and do not represent any of the communities. Apparently, Harner promised to build them homes if they would co-operate with him.

Benitez stated that Harner came to Honduras to pan for gold approximately ten years ago and is well known in the area, although not for working with indigenous communities – something he never did prior to Hurricane Mitch – but rather as a gold 'coyote', or intermediary, because of his dealings in buying and selling gold.

According to the indigenous representatives, the World Food Programme, Catholic Relief Services, the German Co-operation Agency and CARE-Olancho, with the help of the US military at the Soto Cano Air Base, have been giving Harner 'humanitarian' aid to be distributed in coordination with the local municipality. Native leaders said that during the summer of 1999, Harner handled several food shipments in the district but that, according to gold-panners, the donations had been traded for local gold. ❑

William Escofet

CORRECTION

On p160 of The New Slavery (*Index* 1/2000), we stated that *Index on Censorship* had submitted an edited published text of an interview, entitled 'In the battalion', to Christian Aid for confirmation of its authenticity. This statement was incorrect. The article had not been submitted to Christian Aid in any edited or pre-edited form, and we used the name of Christian Aid in error. ❑

TONY GERAGHTY

Tapping into the future

The bugging of Gerry Adams's car shows how the war against the terrorist has turned into a secret war against the citizen

The Irish peace process matters to people beyond the kneecap zone. For Prime Minister Tony Blair the priority is to staunch the waste of the billions expended on the Irish War. For President Clinton – the first man to 'turn' Sinn Fein leader Gerry Adams – the challenge is to win the Irish vote with a programme for peace. For both, the agenda has to be to end the conflict without claiming victory over the IRA even if, in effect, that is what has happened (and explains why the guerrillas will not surrender their arsenal).

What then do we make of the bugging of the Ford Mondeo car used by Adams for his trips to meet IRA chieftains last year? Adams, having exchanged the Armalite for ballot box, is not regarded by republican hardliners as an unmixed blessing. Like the Unionist leader David Trimble, he has a problem of fundamentalists on his own side. The IRA, with its institutionalised paranoia (refreshed by the worming presence of informers) consistently anticipates compromise and betrayal when neither is present. Unsurprisingly, the IRA line on arms decommissioning has steadily hardened since the Adams compromise. He, in self-defence, had to be seen to unmask the risk to which he had inadvertently exposed some of his ambivalent allies. He did so amid tangled wiring and circuit boards at an expertly-managed press conference in December last year.

The sole beneficiaries of an enfeebled peace process will be those whose careers (like those of their Cold War predecessors) seemed secure until the political landscape changed around them. Among seasoned spy-watchers, the surprise was not that the Mondeo was bugged but that the operation was so elaborate. This was not a single voice recorder. It was an orchestra of equipment, the best that Q could manufacture. The beast was about the size and shape of a garden spade, and combined a voice-activated recorder with a satellite tracker to monitor the car's position. Most of the equipment, apart from yards of wire, was expertly installed in the vehicle's roof.

Research for my book *The Irish War* (*Index* 2/1999) had not uncovered anything so elaborate except, perhaps, in a few IRA hideouts or MI5 safe houses, which required a week or so to refit, while the owners were lured away on 'free' holidays, prizes 'won' in obscure competitions. Cars, usually, were fitted with a single microphone installed during a brief overnight job on the target vehicle, while an identical twin was parked in its place, lest the owner happened to wake and check.

The Adams job required reconstruction of much of the car. This was a far cry from the days of 'The Brick', the unwieldy tracing device with its phallic aerial, magnetically attached to target vehicles in the 1970s. At that time, the joke was that you could identify an agent of Box 500 by the plasters covering stigmata-like wounds in one or both palms, caused by the aerial spike in an over-hasty attachment operation, probably on the part of someone rolling beneath the car as it was about to drive away.

Why would a limb – or limbs – of the octopus that is British intelligence feel sufficiently emboldened to continue running its own, separate policy for Northern Ireland? First, there is the encouragement it has received from the control-freak administration of Blair himself. Since New Labour took power, more bugging operations have been authorised than at any time since the end of WWII. The total for 1998 was 1,763, a 3% increase on the preceding record year and well above the 1,682 authorised in 1940, the year of the London Blitz. Even these figures represent less than the true picture. Modern technology enables many more monitors to work, and to be co-ordinated by computer, while one warrant might cover many taps. (This, given the ostensible 'authorisation' granted by Mo Mowlam, is probably what happened in the Adams operation.)

Another reason for James Bond's independence in the matter is that for the intelligence services, the peace process can never be the end of the story. Intelligence gathering and surveillance belong to a separate reality, one in which there is never peace: only the threat implicit or actual. But this case will have been weighed with more than usual respect for the classic intelligence criterion, the Risk versus Gain Equation. Too often, in a culture of *military* intelligence (as Ireland is) macho vanity overrides sense. During the Cold War, such clandestine military operations as that run by the British mission to East Germany – a team known as BRIXMIS – regularly tried, without success, to persuade the boys that it was not smart to play games with the Stasi or the Red Army. Soldiers are conditioned to see the world as a continuing World Cup game that they are obliged to win, or else lose face with their peers. As 1 Para's canteen re-creation of a macabre road-death put it, before Private Clegg was convicted of murder: 'Vauxhall Astra: Built by Robots. Driven by Joyriders. Stopped by "A" Company.'

There is a bigger picture. If Adams and the peace process were not safe from the licenced pirates of military intelligence, who is? Well, no one, really. The military surveillance culture has rubbed off on to civilian life almost without our noticing it.

Examples of this transference, from the war against the terrorist to the war against the citizen, abound. From 1990 until 1998, GCHQ (Government Communications Headquarters) ran Umbra, a covert listening station from a communications tower specially built between two British Telecom microwave stations on a site at Capenhurst, Cheshire. The BT facilities were at the heart of all electronic communications between Britain and Ireland. GCHQ intercepted the transmissions carrying this traffic and scanned it using sophisticated libraries of voice profiles. When Channel 4 exposed the wholesale nature of British interceptions of traffic with Ireland, including Irish government material, there was outrage in Dublin. One example: Whitehall, it was believed, had received advance warning of Dublin's bottom line position in the currency crisis which undermined the Irish punt between September 1992 and January 1993. As Patricia McKenna, an Irish Green Party Euro-MP noted: 'Such a situation poses alarming consequences not just for basic civil liberties in Ireland but also for the Irish economy.'

With its American counterpart – the National Security Agency – GCHQ also runs a worldwide system of intercepts known as Echelon, employed for industrial espionage as well as security. The NSA has its own base at Menwith Hill in Yorkshire, thought to be able to intercept two million messages an hour as part of the Echelon programme, employing its own constellation of satellites to raid our privacy (*Index* 5/1998). As an American specialist in such matters told me recently: 'Its sole purpose is to monitor emails to and from anywhere in the world. The purported justification for this system is the drug "problem". However, it is only another ploy to ingress into what little privacy we have left.'

The proliferation of computerised surveillance covers all aspects of life in modern Britain. Your movements by car are increasingly recorded by roadside Trafficmaster cameras. Motorists who have not paid their road fund licences are to be identified by static cameras and a £400,000 covert camera system, fitted to unmarked cars, which will video and 'read' number plates.

Your rail journeys come under the ubiquitous eye of CCTV. Purchase a ticket to ride with a credit card and the Ministry of Defence may check your Barclaycard account at will to confirm where and when you journeyed – as it did in my case – regardless of civilian status. You are stalked by the state from the moment you use an electronic key to open a hotel door and, as you travel, thanks to the computerised records of that Judas in your pocket, the mobile telephone. Your phone company may provide the police with computerised access to your itemised telephone account, to create a 'tree' of your contacts, without any need for a search warrant or notification.

The use of this invasion of privacy, without the legal protection enjoyed by the Americans and others protected by a written constitution, is justified by reference to serious crime, as in the Bulger and Dando cases. Even if the end justifies the means – a doubtful proposition – the desired end is not always achieved. Police investigating the racial murder of Stephen Lawrence used a miniaturised video camera, hidden in an electric light switch at a house in Eltham to film Neil Acourt brandishing a knife as he boasted about his urge to kill blacks. It did not secure a conviction.

We may expect more bugging, more surveillance, more computerisation to reduce freedoms we took for granted before the Irish War. We have been warned by Straw himself. He reminded a public meeting last May that there were an estimated one million security cameras in stations, streets and shopping centres. On an average day in the big city, most people would be filmed by more than 300 cameras linked to 30 separate CCTV networks. In his eyes, this loss of privacy was 'a price worth paying' for greater security.

MI5 and the other agencies responsible for bugging Gerry Adams would say 'Amen!' to that. ❏

Tony Geraghty is the author of The Irish War *(HarperCollins, 1998). On 23 December the Home Office announced it had dropped the charges that the book breached the Official Secrets Act*

NEIL SAMMONDS

Israel in a spin

Three events in February challenged Israel's preferred role as lone victim in a sea of Arab troubles: first, an admission in the Knesset that Israel possesses nuclear weapons; second, the declassification of a report that found widespread torture of Palestinians during the Intifada; third, the revelation that Israel's claim to be fighting terrorism in South Lebanon not only conflicts with the evidence, but has lost support at home

On 2 February, shattering decades of silence on Tel Aviv's 'nuclear ambiguity', a highly taboo subject, Knesset Member Issam Mahoul initiated the Israeli parliament's first ever debate on its nuclear arsenal. It followed the release in November of 1,200 pages of heavily edited testimony from Mordechai Vanunu, the Israeli nuclear technician who was jailed for 18 years in 1986 for revealing Israel's nuclear secrets to the *Sunday Times*. Mahoul has also called for the release of Mordechai Vanunu, whom he regards as a 'prisoner of conscience, a prisoner of peace, of the struggle for peace'.

Israel has never admitted its possession of nuclear weapons, and writing about them in the press is forbidden unless journalists quote foreign sources or the story has appeared first in the foreign media. Israel has refused to sign the nuclear non-proliferation treaty, and has always forbidden international inspection of its nuclear reactor at Dimona in the Naqab desert. But the Speaker of the Knesset, Avraham Burg, while defending Tel Aviv's policy of ambiguity said he was 'pleased that my decision [to air the issue] opens another area for public discussion'.

Mahoul, an Israeli Arab of the left-wing Hadash group, took the opportunity to accuse successive governments of 'fraud, lies and deceit', in which the media and academics had collaborated 'to brainwash and drug the public'. Mahoul said Israel had stockpiled 'the insane amount of 200 to 300' nuclear weapons and that it was adapting German-built submarines 'to cruise deep in the sea and constitute a second strike force in the event that Israel is attacked with nuclear weapons'. He added that the Dimona nuclear reactor could contaminate the country for centuries, that Israel was producing 'biological warfare' materials at an institute at Nes Tsiona and he criticised the secrecy surrounding the missile sites at Kfar Zechariah near Jerusalem, and Yodfat in the Galilee.

Two dozen right-wing MKs walked out and five Arab MKs were expelled for heckling in a debate which the government only allowed after Mahoul threatened to appeal to the Supreme Court. Speaking on behalf of the Prime Minister Ehud Barak, Haim Ramon said he could not respond as 'to do so would aid the enemy'.

The second revelation unfolded on 9 February when a recommendation by the Supreme Court led to the issue of a carefully edited summary of the Ben-Porat report. Israeli State Comptroller Miriam Ben-Porat studied the practices of Israel's internal intelligence service – Shin Bet – in the Occupied West Bank and Gaza Strip during 1988-92. She presented the report to an intelligence sub-committee of the Parliamentary State Audit Committee in 1997; it suppressed the report, releasing the nine-page edition over two years later.

The summarised report states what Palestinians and human rights organisations have known for years, namely that Israeli security forces were systematically torturing detainees. The forms of torture exceeded the levels of 'moderate physical pressure' permitted by the dubious Landau Commission of 1987: 'Most of the violations were not caused by lack of knowledge of the line between what was permitted and what was forbidden, but were committed knowingly,' the report says.

Ben-Porat singled out the Central Prison in the Gaza Strip where 'veteran and even senior interrogators ... committed severe and systematic deviations'. The leadership knew about the torture but did not intervene. The agents lied about their activities and concocted false reports in court. 'The assurances of senior Shin Bet officials to the Landau Commission that truth-telling inside the organisation is enforced … were found to have no basis in reality,' says the report.

The summary report excludes details of the torture used, but this has been well documented by organisations such as *B'Tselem*, the Israeli human rights group. *B'Tselem* estimates 85% of Palestinian detainees were tortured; ten were killed and hundreds more maimed in the process. The favoured methods were shaking, tying up in excruciating positions, subjecting victims to heat or cold and beating and kicking.

The debate on torture continues among Palestinians as well as Israelis. Bassam 'Eid of the Palestinian Human Rights Group praised Israel's democratic institutions that had made the report possible, adding that its publication was 'better late than never'. Torture has now become common under the Palestinian authorities, he said: 'Those who were tortured by the Israelis have now become the torturers.'

Meanwhile, 47 KMs are backing a bill to reintroduce the ability to use 'moderate pressure' during interrogations; Ehud Barak has set up a committee to examine the issue. *B'Tselem* strongly opposes the initiative. Spokesman Yael Stein said: 'We claimed for years that the minute you allow a little physical pressure you can't limit the amount. Interrogators are quickly going to use methods that are very much more severe.'

While the hawkish element in the Israeli security forces may feel somewhat beleaguered at home, it can still rely on the western media to support its adventures in southern Lebanon. This went true to form in the week after the killing of six Israeli troops in South Lebanon, when Israeli bombs injured 18 civilians and tore apart three power stations, leaving the population with power cuts expected to last over a year, and the government with repair costs of cUS$47m. Israeli Foreign Minister David Levy threatened that the 'soil of Lebanon will burn' if rockets are fired into northern Israel. This was within days of the Knesset's debate on its nuclear and biological weapons.

Despite its disproportionate use of force and focus on civilian targets, Israel still uses the old blackmail to great effect. Israeli spokeman Moshe Fogel justified the raids on the power stations saying: 'Hezbollah terrorists are killing our soldiers and civilians.' Madeleine Albright labelled the Hezbollah 'enemies of peace' and backed up Tel Aviv's allegation that the Hezbollah had attacked from villages, which would have been in contravention of the April 1996 ceasefire accords that forbid attacks on civilian targets or from civilian areas. The Israeli ambassador to the UK wrote that the raids were in response to 'terrorist activities against Israel across the border'. The BBC reported 'the killing of six Israeli soldiers', without mentioning that this was inside Lebanon. There were more features on the 'suffering' of the thousands of northern Israelis forced to spend nights in their bunkers than on the civilian injuries and damage to the infrastructure in Lebanon.

Yet not a single rocket was fired into Israel. Not a single Israeli civilian was injured. UNIFIL commander Timur Goskel stated that the Hezbollah had not violated the accords; Tel Aviv itself said it was suspending them. The Israeli soldiers are part of an occupying force in South Lebanon. Since 1978, UN Resolution 425 has called for their 'immediate and unconditional' withdrawal. Few journalists took time to recall this.

The *Washington Post* referred to Israel's 'intervention' in Lebanon, using, as Robert Fisk points out, the same term the Soviets used for their invasion of Afghanistan. Israeli diplomats were reportedly involved in a letter-writing campaign to newspaper editors explaining away the 'intervention' as a response to 'terrorism', neglecting to mention that the killings were in occupied Lebanon, that those killed were military not civilian and that the 17 civilians injured were all Lebanese.

But where southern Lebanon is concerned, such linguistic and media devices can only paper over widening cracks in Israelis' support for the 22-year-old occupation. The mass-circulation *Yedioth Ahronoth* newspaper published a poll this month indicating that 57% of the public wants an immediate pull-out, without waiting for deals with Beirut and Damascus. *Maariv* reported that only seven members of Barak's 20-strong cabinet believe Israel should wait for peace agreements before withdrawing and it is widely reported that the morale of the frontline troops is at an all-time low. With seven IDF soldiers and two SLA militiamen killed in less than three weeks, pressure for the pull-out is mounting. 'Take the boys out of Lebanon,' reserve colonel Aryeh Itah appealed to Barak after his son was killed by a Hezbollah missile. 'Please do it quickly so that my son Tzahi will be the last sacrifice.' London's *Guardian* reported that Israeli soldiers in the occupation zone were *begging* reporters to 'help us get out of here'. One told Israeli radio: 'You have to be in Lebanon to understand that there is no way we are going to win this war. None of us wants to be the last one killed in it.'

Similar manipulation, or wordplay, is evident in accounts of the troubled Syrian-Israeli talks where President Assad is shown as a 'stubborn old dictator' who won't 'rein in the Hezbollah terrorists' and Barak is the 'man of peace' who's made the negotiations possible. Yet a leaked US document shows that it is Damascus that has been the most conciliatory in talks, while Tel Aviv, for example, will use the word 'redeploy' instead of 'withdraw', and states that the 'redeployment' will exclude civilians. Lebanese politicians have also suggested that Damascus is prepared, despite its public stance that withdrawal to the June 1967 borderline is non-negotiable, to allow for 'adjustment' to facilitate a deal. Sources in Damascus, Beirut and Tel Aviv all concur that a 'full' withdrawal is still likely by the autumn. An adviser to Lebanese Prime Minister Salim Hoss predicted that deals would be concluded before the US presidential elections in November. Nawaf Salam said that Clinton 'will have a grand signing ceremony and win the Nobel prize'. ❑

Neil Sammonds edits Iraqi Sanctions Monitor *and monitors the Middle East for* Index

DMITRY BYKOV

Between a rock and a hard place

Bill Clinton has said the USA can 'do business' with Russia's acting President Vladimir Putin. According to a rising young Russian journalist, there's nothing to choose between him and the rest: they're all villains

The most significant aspect of the recent elections to the Russian *Duma* is that there was no choice. It will be the same in the forthcoming presidential election in March. You can't vote with a clear conscience for any of our politicians since all have proved themselves to be unprincipled in one way or another. The choice in the *Duma* elections was between the OVR, a monstrous grouping of functionaries, bureaucrats and criminals presided over by Yury Luzhkov, mayor of Moscow, and his recently acquired comrade-in-arms, former prime minister Yevgeny Primakov. Virtually indistinguishable from it, only pro-Kremlin, was the Unity or 'Bear' Party behind Putin, Then there was Grigory Yavlinsky, whose much vaunted integrity impelled him to berate the wholly harmless Yeltsin while giving the much more dangerous Luzhkov a gentle slap on the wrist; and a coalition of right-wing forces targetting the 'middle class' and 'fashionable young people', at best the most criminal, at worst the most parasitical segments of Russian society. There was no party representing the average member of the intelligentsia, not a single serious defender of Russia's workers, no one not sullied by alliances with the criminal world or tactical compromises with opponents. Not one principled politician.

The divide in Russian society is not between supporters of Primakov and supporters of Putin, but between those mainly concerned for their reputation and questionable moral purity, and those who proclaim their commitment to the future of Russia in the new century, itself no more compatible with moral purity. Russia is faced with a choice: not between filth and purity, but between two kinds of filth; not between dictatorship and freedom, but between two kinds of authoritarianism.

The opposition of OVR and Kremlin is spurious if for no other reason than that the functionaries and bureaucrats have little moral right to criticise Yeltsin and the so-called 'Family': everything that has gone on in Russia in recent years has been done by these people acting in collusion. The rampant corruption in Moscow rules out taking Luzhkov's criticism of the Kremlin at all seriously, something that was glaringly obvious long before the scandal of the Bank of New York broke. For anybody who has stayed even a month in Moscow and watched the broadcasts emanating from Luzhkov's TV Centre, it has been no less glaringly obvious that his sole reason for deciding to stand for the presidency was that he fell for the immoderate flattery coming, in accordance with Soviet traditions, from among his retinue. And whose head wouldn't be turned by such a torrent of praise? In *Pravda* in 1952, Stalin rated between nine and 12 mentions per issue; in *Vechernyaya*

Moskva today, Luzhkov rates up to 15.

The Kremlin's last chance card for trumping the Luzhkov-Primakov alliance was a bloc of young bully-boys, careerists and fanatics originating, like Primakov himself, in the depths of Russia's intelligence services. In August 1999, the clever money was on this happy few: Vladimir Rushailo, Nikolai Patrushev, Sergei Shoigu and Vladimir Putin. Putin has no merits as a candidate for the presidency other than being prepared to go to any lengths and possessing exceptional physical stamina. Yet the fact that he is relatively young, energetic, mobile to the point of ubiquity and capable of coherent speech, raised Russian hopes.

Throwing their own dubious trump cards into the game, Luzhkov and Primakov accused Putin of being in the financier Berezovsky's pocket. (In the view of OVR, anybody enjoying even the slightest success in opposing Luzhkov and Primakov is in Berezovsky's pocket.) They also alleged that he was not without involvement in the blowing up of apartment blocks in Moscow – as yet an unsolved crime. Given their own record, the accusation that Putin is peculiarly cruel, smacks of desperation. It was, after all, Luzhkov who first spoke of 'cleansing' Moscow in 1996 when two trolleybuses were blown up in the city entrusted to his care. To this day, not a shred of evidence has been produced to substantiate the mayor's assertions of Chechen involvement, Further, several railway carriages full of Caucasians were sent out of Moscow without due process or any great consideration for their human rights after the two apartment blocks were blown up in September 1999. Few people suppose that if Luzhkov were conducting the Chechnya campaign there would be anything left of Chechnya within a month, no matter what the cost in casualties to our troops. As for Luzhkov and Primakov's charge that Putin is preparing to conclude an alliance with the Communists, this is the pot calling the kettle black: the OVR itself said it wouldn't rule out such an alliance and would even work towards it. Primakov went on to remind us that Marx was respected throughout the world and that the communists were one of the constructive forces of our society.

The fact that Putin's opponents are compulsive liars does not, however, give him carte blanche to resort to violence whenever he chooses. His detractors have plenty of ammunition against him if they look: for instance, his unambiguous support for the communist demagogue Gennady Seleznev in the elections for the governorship of

Moscow; his understating of the number of dead in Chechnya, the exclusion of journalists and the distortion of the truth about the war; the complete absence of any programme or outstanding leaders in the pro-Putin Unity Party; and, finally, his all-too-evident readiness to resolve all questions by force – a profoundly Chekist faith in the power of the fist.

I'm inclined to agree with Gleb Pavlovsky, a pro-Kremlin but sharp-witted political commentator, who said that in September 1999 no competent political adviser would have recommended that Putin try to raise his popularity by means of a war in Chechnya. It was obviously much easier to get bogged down in such a war that to bring it to a victorious conclusion. Nevertheless, Putin backed his own judgment, staked his future on war and was proved right.

This was dictated as much by his insight that this was a perfect way of channelling the Russian population's accumulated resentment as by his inherent militarism. The war with Chechnya has been transformed into a war against the dependence and humiliation our ruined country has been suffering for the past eight years. Putin provided a scapegoat for the population's rage, directing it at terrorists (which includes not only practically all Chechens, but also the oligarchs, the corrupt, the functionaries—everybody the people hate and whom the country hopes to overcome with the aid of its new president). It would be difficult to imagine a neater solution.

But if we accept that Putin did not so much want a war as a scapegoat for popular resentment, that hardly makes supporting him more moral. To date, he has come up with no positive proposals; the only thing in his favour is that, unlike Luzhkov and Primakov, he had not, so far, encroached on what remains of our democratic freedoms – though the censorship exercised throughout the war is threatening to equalise the two sides. While the propaganda wars were not started by the Kremlin, they have been carried on shamelessly by both sides.

The choice for Russia in March 2000, as in December 1999 then, is far from appealing. Both sides have abandoned the last vestiges of morality, both play outside the rules when it suits them; while one feels a certain fear or shame at its antics, for the other, violence and corruption are the order of the day. So which side should the Russian voter support? There is nothing to be said in ideological or political terms for Putin, tomorrow's violator and abuser being in no way preferable to yesterday's. Putin's relatively relaxed attitude towards criticism is grounded not in his easygoing nature (as was the case with Yeltsin), but in complete indifference to the 'shrieking and gibbering' of his opponents. Myself, I prefer Putin's brand of authoritarianism to Luzhkov's; in Luzhkov's presence I feel like a pawn in front of a king; in the presence of Putin, I feel part of a monolith capable of accomplishing great things. ❏

Dmitry Bykov *is a weekly columnist for* Sobesednik, *He also contributes to* Novaya gazeta, Obshchaya gazeta *and* Liteeraturnaya gazeta *and is one of Moscow's best-known young poets*
Translated by Arch Tait

NJABULO NDEBELE

The race card

The South African Human Rights Commission claims 'subliminal racism' permeates the country's white-owned press. Editors respond by claiming that press freedom is under attack

Early in December, the Johannesburg weekly *Mail & Guardian* (*M&G*) became involved in a strident exchange with the office of President Thabo Mbeki. It began with an editorial on 10 December accusing the President of running a 'backroom government' and 'threatening to make nonsense' of South Africa's fledgling democracy. These charges prompted an outraged response from Parks Mankahlana, the president's spokesman.

Mankahlana's reaction came in the wake of persistent complaints from many sectors of the public that, since the end of apartheid, the *M&G* has shown disdain for the black-dominated government through biased reporting, slander by innuendo, unsubstantiated allegations of corruption and incompetence, unprofessional annual ratings of government ministers and attacks on the reputations of black public figures. A pattern had emerged which convinced many that the *M&G*

had become a vehicle for the expression of racist anxieties about the future of white South Africans under a black government.

The *M&G* denied these charges, claiming they were a veiled attack on press freedom. But the persistence of racist reporting finally prompted the South African Human Rights Commission (SAHRC), a body established under the terms of the constitution, to undertake a survey of racism in the media. The interim report was released last November to outrage from the editors of several newspapers, including the *M&G*, *Star*, *Cape Argus*, *Cape Times* and the *Sunday Times*. These editors have since been subpoenaed to appear before the SAHRC to answer allegations of 'subliminal racism'.

One thing is certain: for a newspaper that enjoyed solid anti-apartheid credentials, the *M&G* has changed into a right-of-centre voice for disgruntled white liberals. This should come as no surprise. The arrival of democracy has fractured the easy solidarities of the anti-apartheid struggle; South Africans are now free to be who they really are. In this respect, the *M&G* no longer represents any progressive vision of the present or future for many South Africans, regardless of colour. Press freedom is not currently under threat in South Africa. What is under attack is the kind of racism that comes through the columns of the *M&G*. And the exchange between Parks Mankahlana and the newspaper revealed some of the mechanisms by which that racism is articulated.

Mankahlana's response to the *M&G*'s editorial on 10 December did not fit editor Philip van Niekerk's riposte in his follow-up editorial on 17 December. It was neither 'hysterical' nor 'tawdry'; it did not 'resort to emotional racial invective'; nor was it a descent 'into paranoid nonsense about natives and basket cases'. Rather than being a 'dangerous display of defensive arrogance', it was a pained attempt to get the *M&G* seriously to consider becoming a credible source of information and intelligent commentary.

Mankahlana began with a point-by-point refutation of the *M&G*'s allegations about Mbeki's political conduct. His point was that a responsible newspaper could not claim that the government was 'threatening to make nonsense of our democracy' without deploying a good deal of verifiable evidence and persuasive analysis. Van Niekerk conceded that Mankahlana had made 'some good points which we accept in the spirit of debate', without indicating which these were, as opposed to those that remained in contention.

When the editor of a serious paper proclaims the 'right to be wrong', as the *M&G* did in its 17 December editorial, it does nothing for reader confidence. Such a right, if it exists, has to be earned and to earn it a newspaper has to demonstrate a consistent record of integrity in its reporting, commentaries and analyses. Without that record, the 'right to be wrong' becomes the right to misinform, defame, scandalise and exploit through damaging innuendo, all in the name of the 'free flow of criticism and debate' – and, of course, selling papers.

There have been other cries of agony recently from individuals and institutions that felt unfairly treated by the *M&G*. Barney Cohen, chief executive of Urban Brew Studios, complained on 10 December about what appeared to him to be a 'campaign of slander' by the *M&G* 'achieved by using unsubstantiated information from a vindictive inside informant'. After revealing further inaccuracies, Cohen appealed: 'It's about time we put end to highly damaging speculation and innuendo.'

In an article on 10 December headlined 'Principal raises his pay', the paper reported that Attie Buitendacht, vice chancellor of Technikon SA, 'gave himself a 35% salary increase' and, in doing so, 'neglected to seek the governing council's approval,' an act which allegedly forced the chair of council to resign. In its response, Technikon revealed that the increase was approved and the chair had, in fact, not resigned. The *M&G* has still failed to correct the error. The headline's implication that Buitendacht had engaged in corrupt conduct has been left in place to wreak havoc on his reputation. The newspaper doesn't care. 'The right to be wrong' is out of control.

The second part of Mankahlana's response sought to understand why a supposedly reputable publication consistently gets its facts wrong; routinely fails to verify and investigate the authenticity of its sources; displays a persistent inability to 'balance' the evidence; and routinely fails to publish the defence of those it targets for exposure and damns by innuendo.

Van Niekerk should have answered some of Mankahlana's questions. Was it true that the *M&G* had 'virulently opposed the Pan African Congress and Azapo accepting the offer to participate' in Nelson Mandela's government? Was it true that the *M&G* later suggested that the Democratic Party's (DP) participation would be 'in the national interest?' If so, then surely van Niekerk was obliged to explain the basis on which his newspaper had preferred the participation of one group against that of another.

If *M&G*'s Howard Barrell writes in his column that the DP 'may *also* be led by a bunch of venal, ambitious, self-serving bastards', is it not the legitimate right of any reader to ask who the other 'bastards' might be? If Mankahlana was wrong to suggest who, in his opinion, these 'bastards' really were, then van Niekerk should have demonstrated why this was so.

Given our history of racism, is it unreasonable to suspect racism behind an inconsistency in which the option for a white party, in place of black ones, remains unexplained? In the same way, it is not unreasonable for a reader to fill in the missing term in the syllogism involving Howard Barrell's 'bastards'? Van Niekerk's heated response strongly suggested that Mankahlana had touched a nerve.

I concede that many white South Africans find themselves in an invidious position when they sense that the racist card is being raised to silence them. There are many black South Africans who will be tempted to use that card with effect. White South Africans must learn to recognise when the card is being exploited, and deal with it appropriately. Otherwise, they will be charged with crying 'Racism' whenever it suits them. The resort to evasion rather than argument results in ridiculous postures intended to demonstrate that there is at least one white man who cannot be intimidated.

Van Niekerk has a penchant for shifting the terms of discussion in an attempt to undermine a respondent's arguments on grounds other than their substance. This he invariably does under the heading: 'The Editor Replies'. He disingenuously invites readers to take his side when he poses a heavily loaded question: 'Is the criticism of the presidency the same as an attack on the country's new democracy? What do you think?' First, this question strongly suggests that the issue it raises is, in fact, a position held by Mankahlana. This is false. Second, it pretends to initiate a serious inquiry when it already contains its own answer: a resounding 'No!' As a tactic, this represents the ultimate disrespect for the public intellect.

Van Niekerk is unable to distinguish between the act of criticism, which is not under attack, and the content of criticism, which Mankahlana legitimately challenges. Failure to recognise this distinction apparently leads him to accuse Mankahlana of what he himself does routinely. The *M&G* consistently equates criticism of itself with an attack on press freedom. Van Niekerk deploys this argument in his assault on the Human Rights Commission's decision to call for a study on racism and the media. Surely he should accept the logic of his own argument: that presidency and press should be beyond criticism. Strangely, he votes for the immunity of the press, but not of the presidency. We are faced with another baffling inconsistency.

But what do we make of habitual inconsistency; of uncritical reliance on rumour and leaked documents as sources of information; of headlines that have no bearing on the substance of an article? I suggest that what we are facing here is something serious. We witness not only the decline of professionalism, but a profound failure of the intellect.

This prompts some important questions:

What is the process by which a newspaper determines its editorial stance? Who is involved in the process of determining it?

What understanding of social transformation informs its formulation? How does it influence strategies of representation?

How are the resulting representations of society contested and negotiated with the reading public that responds to them?

More crucial, does the newspaper have sufficient and diverse intellectual resources to answer these questions?

Can it transcend methods of representation trapped in outmoded yet subliminally powerful intellectual paradigms?

Does it have the capacity to interrogate itself?

One thing is clear: we need to move forward. The mandate of journalism in today's South Africa urgently needs revision. Public confidence needs to be restored in a sector that has a responsibility to project more complex images of our society. We need a press that is trustworthy; that deepens public knowledge, enriches social insight, nurtures a vigorous and courageous atmosphere of public discussion and, above all, respects its public. ❏

Njabulo Ndebele is the author of Fools & Other Stories *and critical essays on South African literature and culture. He is currently Scholar-in-Residence at the Ford Foundation in New York. He submitted a version of this article to the* Mail & Guardian, *which declined to publish it*

Dear *Index* reader,

ITN v *LM* court case starts 28 February 2000!
We need your help.

As you may know, ITN is suing *LM* magazine for libel, over a story about ITN's award-winning pictures of a Bosnian camp published in the February 1997 issue. The case is due to start in the High Court on 28 February and we need your support to fight it.

For the past three years, ITN's libel writs have been hanging over the magazine. The case has already cost us tens of thousands of pounds in legal fees and expenses—money that should have been spent on expanding and improving *LM*. Now, if we lose in court, we are faced with the threat of bankruptcy. The case has broader implications for press freedom in this country.

As you read this the meter is running on our legal costs. To fight this case, and defend press freedom, we desperately need your help.

Many Friends of *LM*, as well as eminent writers, journalists, academics and artists, have already supported the *LM* defence fund. Make a donation today, using the form below. Please give as much as you can afford for free speech.

Yours sincerely,

MICK HUME, Editor, *LM*   HELENE GULDBERG, Co-publisher, *LM*

WE NEED YOUR HELP

To keep up to date with the case, go to http://www.informinc.co.uk/ITN-vs-LM/

I have enclosed a donation of: ☐ £10 000   ☐ £1000   ☐ £500   ☐ £300   ☐ £100   ☐ Other £

Name:

Address:

Postcode:

Make cheques payable to Off the Fence Fund. Send donation to:
Off the Fence, c/o *LM* magazine, Signet House, 49-51 Farringdon Road, London, EC1M 3JP.

☐ Please tick box or indicate if you do not wish to be publicly thanked in print for your donation.

HELENE GULDBERG

The perils of nuance

Even more than a Freedom of Information Act, the UK needs a change in its biggest gagging device – the world's most draconian libel laws

Welcome to London, libel capital of the world. The capital's High Court attracts chancers from around the world who know that the odds are overwhelmingly in favour of those who sue. For a start, libel law rests upon the assumption that the claimant has an 'unblemished record'. In addition, those who sue do not have to prove actual harm. They need only show that the words complained of are *capable* of lowering their public standing. Nor do claimants need to prove that the words complained of are untrue. It is presumed that the defamatory statement is false and the burden therefore falls on the defendant to prove its truth – a reverse burden of proof almost unique to English libel law.

That is not all. The defendant not only has to defend the literal meaning, but any possible interpretation or unintended meaning. To argue that a particular defamatory meaning was not intended will not hold up in court. No wonder claimants succeed in over 80% of cases. With those odds the libel courts provide rich pickings – but only for the wealthy since the costs involved frequently amount to six- or seven-figure sums.

The most worrying aspect of the UK libel law is the chilling effect it has on free speech. If authors, editors or publishers have the smallest doubt that the truth of a proposition cannot be proven in court (even when made in good faith), the story is usually dropped. One never knows what may emerge in the discovery process or how witnesses, on either side, will perform in the witness box.

In other countries some attempt is made to strike a balance between the right of free speech and the right to defend one's reputation. The landmark US ruling of *New York Times v Sullivan* in 1964 created a public-figure defence, making it very difficult for public individuals to sue. To succeed, claimants would need to show that not only were the allegations untrue, but that they were made with reckless disregard for the truth. The Supreme Court observed that in free debate erroneous statements are inevitable and must be protected – otherwise free expression will not have the 'breathing space' it needs and media self-censorship will be inevitable.

The basic principles of English libel law have survived most attempts at reform. In 1774 Lord Mansfield stated: 'Whatever a man publishes he publishes at his peril.' His statement could equally be applied to English libel law at the start of the twenty-first century. A recent ruling in the House of Lords appeared to offer newspapers some relief, recognising that 'the press discharges vital functions as a bloodhound as well as a watchdog'. Newspapers will be able to invoke a special defence of 'qualified privilege' in libel actions if information is so important that public interest outweighs the right to safeguard reputation.

However, the criteria that need to be met to qualify for the protection inevitably result in the submission of editorial judgments to judicial scrutiny. The factors taken into account include the seriousness of the allegation, the source of the information, the steps taken to verify the information, the urgency of the matter and the tone of the article. They are all rather vague. Editors will not know at the time of publication whether a particular story is likely to be protected or not – and are more likely to drop it than take the chance.

As someone at the receiving end of a writ, facing bankruptcy if the claimant succeeds, I am acutely aware of the costly and time-consuming nature of libel trials. But the law affects not only those journalists, broadcasters, editors and publishers who are faced with libel writs. It has a chilling effect on the whole media. Nobody wants to be dragged into years of legal wrangling, lawyers' meetings, evidence gathering and possible cross-examination by a giant of the courtroom. ❏

Helene Guldberg is co-publisher of LM magazine. She is co-defendant in ITN's libel action against LM and legal co-ordinator of LM's libel defence

Women who censor

When sex rears its head, universal sisterhood flies out of the window. We look at the disagreements and cultural differences over pornography, sex and violence, the right to abortion and the veiling of women, and confront the women who believe in censorship as a means of protecting themselves, their daughters and their culture

File compiled by Elizabeth Wilson

ELIZABETH WILSON

Women who censor

Women have never been politically united. One of the reasons for the opposition to female suffrage in the USA and Britain in the nineteenth century was the fear that, enfranchised, women would form their own parties to pursue their own interests – interests that might be inimical to men. Once the vote had been won, however, women diversified, fragmented, went their separate ways. Interests based on class, ethnicity, religion, motherhood, employment and attitudes to sex proved more important than a common sense of gender identity.

This history was repeated in the 1960s and early 1970s. Second-wave feminism or women's liberation at first based itself on the Utopian idea of universal sisterhood – the interest of all women across classes, across races, across the globe. But this soon caused internal dissent, attacked as a racist attempt by privileged white women to dominate the agenda and the movement. African-American women could not feel sisterly towards white women whose great-grandmothers had presided over cotton plantations worked by cohorts of slaves. Minority women in Britain felt that a history of imperialist oppression, in which many white women had willingly participated, was being ignored. Class differences, too, were painful and difficult. Women with children felt that the 'child-free' did not understand their fearful dilemmas, the parcelling up of their day between children, paid work and domestic drudgery, but lesbians equally felt that their sexuality was belittled or denied.

Given these diverse histories, it is astonishing that feminism has made so much progress. While this issue of *Index on Censorship* focuses on divisions among women, it is important to remind ourselves that women collectively achieved much in the century just past, whether or not they called themselves feminists. It is, however, also important to confront differences between women. This is because in a world of mass media, complex issues get turned into headlines, become the focus of short-term hysteria and then suffer extinction. Yet the feelings behind the headlines do not go away, and demand a more subtle process of understanding. In different ways, women's position is as vulnerable and uncertain as it ever was – worldwide, for example, the majority of the poor are women. Without an informed analysis of the reasons for their exclusion from health, from education, from a fair share of wealth their situation cannot be improved. Part of this analysis must be of the different and sometimes mutually exclusive ways in which different groups of women have understood the reasons for women's inequality and subordination.

The struggle for women's equality came out of the Enlightenment. It was – and is – associated with the idea that the individual has the right to freedom, to equality before the law and in civil society and as part of a democratic agenda. It therefore springs from the same set of principles as the belief in the right to free speech and the right to freedom of association.

In the nineteenth century, that meant women's right to speak at all and their right to act in the public sphere. In the US in 1848, women were forced to address the Seneca Falls conference from behind a curtain – the very idea of women speaking in public was considered shocking. Before WWI, suffragists fought for the vote because they believed it would give them a public voice in the political arena.

The women's liberationists of the 1970s were concerned with similar rights. They were, as earlier generations of feminists had been, determined to break the silences imposed on women by society – or rather, as many feminists felt, by men. Yet although it shared a number of preoccupations with feminist movements of an earlier time, the women's movement of the 1970s was very much of *its* time too. In particular, it was part of the growing openness in discussions of sexuality and related, previously taboo subjects. Women's writing and campaigning brought into the open the reality of domestic violence, rape and sexual abuse, but these were issues that had, after all, concerned nineteenth-century feminists. Now, women also made more upfront positive demands for sexual experience, sexual diversity and sexual fulfilment. At the same time feminist artists demanded the right to show works that shocked the sensibilities of viewers, exploring body parts, wombs, menstruation, childbirth and other uncomfortable realities. These were at once in danger of being judged 'obscene'. (One possible original meaning of 'obscene' is 'that which is, or should be, hidden'.)

Women were acceptable if young, nubile and passive objects of the male gaze but, unless defined in masculine terms, the female body and female sexuality were still taboo, threatening and unwelcome. When women demanded the right to define and determine their own sexual being and sexual desires, they aroused horror and open aggression. The right to determine their own sexuality therefore became a central demand for feminists of the 1970s.

Yet it was on this very issue that the feminist movement foundered, so fiercely did women disagree – and central to the disagreement was censorship, for the battle that raged among feminists in the 1980s was about pornography. This battle was important, not only because it caused the women's movement to fragment and collapse, but also because it raised issues that have since gained wider purchase, becoming part of the debate on political correctness in the 1980s and 1990s.

There is no agreed definition of pornography, although it is usually accepted that pornography intends to arouse the reader or viewer sexually, and the bottom line would be that it consists of 'sexually explicit material'. British censorship laws define 'obscene' materials as those that 'tend to deprave and corrupt', but sometimes juries have declared pornography obscene and sometimes they haven't. There have been numerous attempts to distinguish between 'erotica' (good) and 'pornography' (bad) but, like all definitions of porn, there is an inescapably subjective dimension to this. Pornography is controversial because sex is controversial. For all the apparent openness of contemporary culture, sex has not lost its power to disturb: there are competing definitions of what pornography 'is' because these reflect deep-seated conflicts about the purpose and role of sex in modern society.

The anti-porn campaign was largely confined to the US, where it originated, and the UK. It gained less purchase in Europe, where perhaps the Roman Catholic sensibility in France and Italy produced a different reaction; Germany and Scandinavia, too, seemed freer of Anglo-Saxon puritanism.

Following the publication of Andrea Dworkin's *Pornography: Men Possessing Women,* the anti-porn campaign soon attracted a section of the feminist movement in Britain, but took a less legalistic form. Women demonstrated outside cinemas showing Brian De Palma's *Dressed to Kill,* a 'slasher' movie, and tried to get it banned. One or two groups took

*Edinburgh, 1990. Women protest against magazine wholesaler
John Menzies forcing shops to stock pornographic magazines –
Credit: Scottish Women Against Pornography*

direct action against shops selling pornography; others used leaflets and
demonstrations to gain wider support.

As in the US, the campaign was also taken up outside the women's
movement, but whereas in the US the Right had appropriated the anti-
porn initiative, in Britain it was the left wing of the Labour Party. This is
less surprising than might appear. The Labour Party, after all, had strong

roots in Methodist evangelicalism. Its Fabian wing had never been
primarily concerned with liberal freedoms but rather with the regulation
of society in ways consistent with a rather utilitarian, and sometimes
even authoritarian, view of socialism. Although, therefore, right-wing
fundamentalism has had relatively little influence in Britain, the anti-
porn campaign was attractive to a Labour Party that felt it would be a
popular, pro-women move to support it.

Two women Labour MPs, Clare Short and Dawn Primarola, took up
the cudgels against porn, attempting, ultimately without success, to drive
private member bills through the House of Commons. Clare Short tried
to get the titillating 'page 3 girl' banned from the tabloid *Sun* – a direct
form of censorship. Dawn Primarola mounted a campaign to have soft-
porn mags such as *Playboy* removed from ordinary newsagents and
confined to special shops. Clare Short's campaign in particular touched a
chord with large numbers of women, and she received several thousand
letters of support. One described how humiliated and upset its writer
felt after a mastectomy by the sight of her husband leering at semi-naked
women over the cereal each morning.

The anti-porn campaigns expressed the anger of large numbers of
women who hated the vulgarity of sexualised images of women
throughout mass culture (whether actually pornographic or not) and the
exploitative attitude towards women such images implied. Those women
on both sides of the Atlantic and from across a wide political spectrum
who supported these initiatives felt that exploitation and the contempt
for women implied by such images could be addressed by a quick fix
solution of censorship. The political question was less whether sexually
explicit material was a good or a bad thing in itself – although there
were fundamental conflicts about that as well – than what strategy could
best forward the interests of women. Lynne Segal explores these
complexities.

The political campaigns addressed – or failed to address –
fundamental divisions and disagreements as to what the 'interests of
women' are. Women from deeply polarised positions have claimed to
speak for 'all women' – as happened in the anti-porn debate – but these
claims were not confined to the controversy surrounding explicit sexual
material. By the 1980s feminism had made an impact not only in the
West, but also across the world so that almost any position on a wide
range of matters concerning women was likely to be defended on the

grounds that it was in the interests of women.

Fundamentalist religions, for example, were militant in the propagation of views and practices that might at first seem to contradict an emancipation agenda, but which could be defended on precisely these grounds – however specious such arguments might sometimes appear. It could be difficult for women in the West to oppose such views. In the 1979 revolution in Iran large numbers of women were extremely militant and were found at the forefront of the demonstrations that toppled the Shah. At that point they adopted the veil as a symbol of their rejection of the authoritarian regime of the Shah, and believed that the revolution would improve their position. In this they were supported by the then views of the Ayatollah Khomeini, who had, when in exile, written and spoken in favour of women's social advancement. The American feminist Kate Millett's widely publicised intervention at the time, when she urged Iranian women not to return to the veil, was taken as an example of American imperialism and racism. It was an inappropriate and insensitive attempt to prioritise the issues that white western women considered important, and showed little insight into how Iranian women themselves saw the situation. Nevertheless, as Maryam Tavakol explains, that did not mean that Iranian women expected or welcomed their subsequent relegation to a wholly subordinate role. This was only one example of the way in which an accusation of racism or 'Islamophobia' could be used to delegitimise the opinions of (white western) women who spoke out against fundamentalist practices.

In the 1980s there was a growing recognition within the British left and in liberal circles in the USA of the racism that was endemic throughout society and which had infected even liberal and socialist thought. Many white feminists were legitimately criticised for their failure to address the needs of women from ethnic minorities and even for their blindness to the very existence of such minorities with distinct sets of interests. Yet this could act as a form of censorship in itself, since it meant that white women were (perhaps rightly) inhibited from raising issues such as forced marriages and genital mutilation which, within western societies, affected mainly minority women.

Feminists in the 1970s believed that to be effective politics must be based on personal experience. No women had the right to speak for others whose experience had been different – only women from the

Asian community in Britain, for example, could appropriately lead a campaign against domestic violence within that community. The women's group, Southall Black Sisters, has campaigned on this issue for many years. In 1999 a (white) woman Labour MP took up the issue of forced marriages among the Asian constituents of her Yorkshire constituency. However, it was even more difficult for her than for Southall Black Sisters in west London to gain a hearing. There was a blanket denial from male leaders of the community that a problem even existed. And women as well as men within minority communities fear with good reason that such campaigns feed racism, reinforce stereotypes and further undermine minority cultures that are already vulnerable. These fears have even, as *Index on Censorship (1/2000)* recently reported, occasionally resulted in tragedy, when a mother has turned against a daughter who has refused to acquiesce in an unwanted marriage, or, worse, has formed a relationship with a man outside her community. Young women have even been murdered for thus dishonouring their families, although such cases are rare. Yet however unusual, they illustrate all too vividly that considerations of family loyalty and the defence (it is felt) of an embattled community whose customs are under threat can appear more important to women (in this case, mothers) than individual freedom. Mothers, grandmothers, mothers-in-law and sisters within these communities act, sometimes in extreme ways, to enforce the rules of their culture on young women (and men) who rebel. They reject liberal western culture, which they feel has abrogated responsibility for children, has undermined children's respect for parents and older people and has weakened such traditional forms of authority within the family as women had. In arguing for voluntary arranged marriages, parents can point to the high rates of family break-up in western societies and scorn the idea that the creation of a family should be based entirely on romantic passion and a sexual attraction that is likely to wane in time. On the other hand, where both young and older women feel threatened, there is little room for debate, and there can be a denial that problems even exist, which is itself a form of censorship.

Western culture is, of course, wide open to criticism on feminist and other grounds. Muslims, for example, sometimes defend the veil and what are seen as other restrictions on Muslim women in public, on the grounds that the only alternative is the super-exploitative and over-sexualised mass culture of the West. Their critique is similar to some of the arguments advanced by American and British anti-porn feminists, even if they reach different conclusions.

Germaine Greer has argued that western feminists must address the misogyny of their own culture. She has attacked the way in which a preoccupation with practices such as female genital cutting (clitoridectomy) can act as a form of censorship-by-denial of equally misogynistic medical practices in western culture. In an article in the *Evening Standard* (10 December 1999) she argued that 'we have been cutting and burning genital tissue for generations, in unnecessary interventions connected with contraception, abortion, childbirth, sterilisation and now IVF'. She went on to argue that 'before we can attack irrational practices in other cultures we have at least to recognise their prevalence in our own'. She also suggested that we westerners should listen to what infibulated women say about their own bodies, referring to themselves as 'closed' women 'who must be "opened" for childbirth and then reclosed. They are often extremely distressed to be told that under British protocols they may not be stitched up as tightly as they wish after being vaginally delivered.' Greer points to the inconsistency of being shocked by such priorities when in this country women are often given unnecessary episiotomies in order to make them 'nice and tight for their husbands'.

We should not be surprised when women, however conservatively, place a greater value on the traditions of their own culture than on personal freedom, since for each of us personal identity is so deeply bound up with culture. There are undoubtedly women (and men) who would rather that such difficult issues were not discussed. Yet it is precisely this aspect of censorship that itself requires discussion.

Dienobou Sanoussa's testimony from Burkina Faso highlights the terrible problems that result from the censorship of silence, as does, in a different context, Judith Levine's account of the alarming forms that censorship of information has taken in the USA. There, Christian fundamentalists have prevented the young – most in need of this information – from having access to information on abortion and contraception. Their influence has also led to the removal of such books as Judy Blume's novels for teenagers from library shelves.

If the censorship of silence and denial is insidious, direct censorship, on grounds of 'political correctness', can also be hard to combat. The history of art in the West (but not exclusively in the West) is a long history of struggle for the right to free expression, and the 'culture wars' that raged through America in the 1980s concerned the right of artists, such as Robert Mapplethorpe, to freedom of expression within a supposedly individualist liberal culture. It is therefore paradoxical that feminists, who have fought so long for the right to a voice of their own, have been complicit in the censorship of works of which they disapprove. For example, at one American university women objected to the display of a Goya painting, the *Naked Maja,* on the grounds that it was offensive to women. In a more recent incident at the British Library in London, women staff members objected to a medallion of a naked Hindu goddess, placed on the wall of their canteen as a form of decoration. Opponents of this kind of political correctness have argued that the removal of everything that might offend anyone must lead to an anodyne and infantilised culture in which debate becomes impossible.

The women who demanded the removal of the Hindu goddess may well have been correct in their view that no similar representation of a naked man would have been used as decoration in that way, and indeed, the representation of the erect male member is as taboo as ever in the West. It is difficult to unravel the feminist dimension of the debate from puritanism on the one hand and from a dislike of the way in which sex is trivialised in western culture on the other. The representation of the Hindu goddess, after all, was not meant just as a decoration, but originally had important spiritual and religious meanings.

Prudishness, feminist resentment at the way women are treated and depicted, and the fear that often lies behind censorship are tangled together. Caught between the anything-goes amorality of consumer culture and the legacy of a repressive past, women have a difficult balance to maintain. The 'pornography wars' of the 1980s exemplified these difficulties. Perhaps we can now move on from the impasse to renew the debate on different terms. ❏

Elizabeth Wilson was active in the women's movement in the 1970s and 80s. She is professor of culture at the University of North London and the author of several books including The Sphinx in City *and the forthcoming* Bohemia: Rebellion as Lifestyle

LYNNE SEGAL

Pornographic battles

Feminists who want to censor pornography claim that it causes
sex crimes. The truth is quite otherwise

Within feminism, battles over pornography have become the wars
without end. We thought it had peaked in the USA in the 1980s,
but the cannons are still firing. Despite the controversy their campaigns
generate, those who see pornography as pivotal to women's oppression
have built a popular base for anti-pornography feminism, and continue
to make inroads into legal frameworks. This is why the issue of
'pornography' will not go away. From the close of the 1970s, it became
impossible to write about sexuality, as a feminist, without being hijacked by, and forced to take a stand on, the issue of pornography.

It has become a disturbingly deadlocked debate. I have been
positioned as part of the 'pro-sex brigade', yet we – opponents of the
theories of the anti-pornography campaigners – have the least titillating
lines. We are always forced to address an agenda which is not of our own
making. The deadlock is hard to shift because the dispute, although
superficially about evidence that pornography is harmful, is ultimately
about competing feminist explanations for women's subordination and
the place given to men and their sexuality as the root of women's
oppression. Whether insisting that sexism does not reduce to the sexual,
or that the meanings of images do not exist independent of their
audience and context, those of us who oppose anti-pornography
feminism have to keep arguing the boring case of 'sweet reason': to insist
on complexity. This is a world apart from the fire and brimstone of anti-
pornography feminism, whose leading theoretician, Catherine
MacKinnon, and maestro of rhetoric, Andrea Dworkin, hit us with their

pounding, repetitive prose and their sadistic sexual imagery to produce a type of passion seemingly all their own, but actually derived from evocative puritan barnstorming down through the ages. The one thing which pornographers and anti-pornographers have in common is the desire to arouse and shock: sexual denunciation, like the anti-masturbation rants of old, provides vicarious outlet for sexual passion, as well as for sexual fears and anxieties.

Whatever the rhetorical interplay between pornography and anti-pornography, it is impossible to deny that the term is slippery. Over the years, its meanings shift and its productions diversify. 'Pornography', in its most widely accepted sense, always flaunts its illicit status: its existence as material designed primarily for sexual arousal, without redeeming social importance. The feminist Linda Williams has mapped the continuous changes in pornographic productions, as new sexual questions and anxieties come into play. In the early stag films of the 1920s the question of women's sexual pleasure was never an issue: men gawped at the forbidden display of female genitals (in screenings from which women were strictly excluded). In contrast, full-length porn movies from the 1980s purport to represent both men and women as sexual subjects, and the issue of satisfying women's (supposedly insatiable) desire drives the plot forward.

Misogyny unquestionably pervades much of the genre. Yet one of the main changes in recent decades has been the targeting of women as well as men as consumers of 'adult videos'. Launched in the USA, self-consciously pro-women pornographic outfits – like Candida Royalle's 'Femme Productions' or Annie Sprinkle's 'Post-Porn Performances' – have emerged, attempting to subvert sexism and portray female sexual agency in a positive light. The latter all routinely encounter the censor's firm hand, both in the USA and, when imported, here. Today it would seem truer than ever that the borders of the 'pornographic' shift and blur into other genres (the uncontrolled, non-commercial productions of nerds on the Internet creating endless new possibilities, and problems). Meanwhile, much of what anti-pornography feminists refer to as classic instances of 'pornography' are taken from the slasher and horror movie genre, with its own distinct history and ways of reading imagery and text.

However, despite all the changes in the genre, it still remains men who predominantly produce and consume most of the sexually explicit images of women (or men). Stock top-shelf 'wank-mags' cater overwhelmingly for men. Attempts to produce somewhat similar porn mags for women have had little commercial success. Here, as nowhere else in most men's lives, infantile grandiosity is fully catered for: men are inexaustibly desiring, tumescent and irresistible; women insatiably available. Whether we respond with derision, sympathy, horror or indifference to what this suggests about men's ruling sexual trepidations will influence the stand we take on pornography.

In the women's liberation movement of the 1970s the analysis and politics of sexuality were always accorded a central place. Feminists initially sought to celebrate female sexuality: liberating it from male-centred discourses and sexist practices to uncover women's own 'autonomous' sexuality. However, early ideas linking women's liberation to greater sexual confidence were soon overshadowed by the pressure of challenging the seeming tenacity of men's power over women. From the close of the 1970s, forceful feminist writing was insisting that predatory male sexuality was the overriding source of that power, and naming pornography as its chief incitement. Male 'sexuality' was irrevocably fused to 'domination', redefined as an urge to power.

Other feminists, as I did, saw these moves as part of a reaction to more conservative times and the setbacks faced by feminist activism – especially in the USA, where anti-pornography feminism arose at the close of the 1970s. Isolating sexuality and men's violence from other issues of women's inequality was not only a defensive tactic for women, but one closest to the rising tide of conservative backlash against radical politics generally. The Right has always liked to demonise sexuality, seeing it as the source of all our ills. Some feminists were now joining them.

The new feminist discourses against pornography were strengthened in 1987 when Catherine MacKinnon published *Feminism Unmodified: Discourses on Life and Law*. This added legal arguments to Andrea Dworkin's earlier indictment of pornography in *Pornography: Men Possessing Women*, published in 1981, which depicted pornography as men's literal domination and torture of women. MacKinnon declared pornography a 'violation of women's civil rights', arguing that it convinces men that women are inferior. Pornography should be seen as not merely a form of representation – sexist and offensive images or words – but as *literally* harming women and creating gender inequality. It

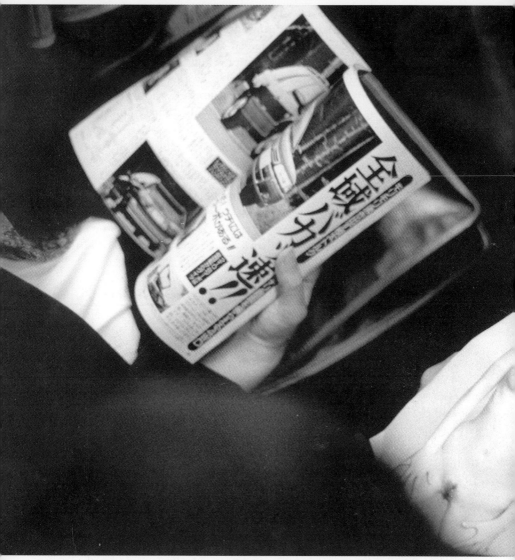

Tokyo, a crowded bullet train. The normalisation of porn –
Credit: Dean Chapman/Panos

causes men to injure and violate women both in its creation (a claim
passionately and repeatedly rebutted by many sex workers themselves)

and in its consumption: teaching men to injure and debase women through linking their sexual arousal to degrading images of women.

The women's liberation movement was not concerned primarily with censorship, either for or against. Rather, feminists saw cultural production of all kinds as a site for feminist struggle to authorise and encourage silenced voices. That said, feminist anti-pornography arguments are seductive because most mainstream pornography purveys blatantly sexist (and often racist) imagery. Pornography's standard servicing of men's narcissistic fantasies of female sexual availability is a continuing provocation when sexual harassment and rape remain endemic. It seems to offer a convenient scapegoat for rage against such abuses. Convenient, but hazardous.

It is hazardous because the argument that it is commercial pornography that underlies the subordination and abuse of women in society is seriously misleading. First of all, anti-pornography feminism has systematically misrepresented the content of mainstream pornography as 'violence'. Secondly, it has consistently misrepresented studies of effects of pornography, falsely claiming they offer consistent and conclusive proof that pornographic images cause sex crimes. Thirdly, it disavows our knowledge of the peculiar nature of fantasy, with its complex, often contradictory, relation to actual behaviour. Fourthly, it eschews recent theories of representation, which reveal that meaning is seen as never simply fixed in advance, but determined by its broader discursive context as well as its specific interpretive audience.

Finally, and most fundamentally of all, anti-pornography feminism fails to address the elementary point that the role of commercial pornography in depicting a crude, imperious and promiscuous male sexuality, alongside female receptivity and vulnerability, is *completely* overshadowed by, and *entirely* dependent on, the official discourses and imagery of science, medicine, religion and mainstream cultural productions (high or low), prevalent all around us.

While many may find the sexually explicit messages of commercial pornography offensive, in fact they mimic – yet also sometimes unsettle – the ways in which the most authoritative, revered, even sacred discourses of our culture depict women as subordinate, sexually passive and sexually available. There have, for example, been feminist critiques of the 'great' paintings of western art along these lines, and illustrations could be drawn from a whole range of genres. Many fields of knowledge rely on a taken-for-granted view of unalterable gender difference that does, in the end, imply the subordination of women. This is nowhere more prominent than in the recent flowering of 'new evolutionary theory', which flaunts its account of men's ever-ready sexual desire. Yet as sex therapists are all too well aware, the sexist metaphors and phallic hubris, both of recent scientific discourse and of traditional pornography, are far from reflecting a real world in which the male member is permanently erect and endlessly ready for unencumbered sex.

In her recent analysis of pornography, *Excitable Speech: A Politics of the Performative*, Judith Butler explores this failure of expectations. She suggests that pornography depicts just those 'unrealizable positions' that predetermine our social expectations of gender behaviour. Pornography in no way constructs that social reality; on the contrary, it serves to mock the impossible distance between gender norms and actual practices.

Nobody needs pornography to remind them of the hierarchical 'truths' of sexual difference. Some, indeed, turn to it to escape them, identifying with who-knows-what position of domination or subjection as they gaze upon its products. It is dominant ideology itself, with its obsessive disdain for what it regards as the gross material body and its functions – of secretions, odours and open orifices; perspiration, pulpy flesh and fluctuating organs – which works to produce the quite inevitable pull of the tauntingly illicit.

Pornography is thus only one of many phallocentric and misogynistic discourses that fashion our images of gender and sexuality – and the least esteemed, least convincing, often most contradictory one. Those who most eagerly insist on its unique offensiveness face the problem that surveys of what is packaged as pornography show that violent imagery is rare, rather than definitive of the genre, as anti-porn feminists claim. Moreover, men are more likely than women to be depicted as 'submissive' in the S&M or bondage imagery available. This means, of course, that were there any truth in our direct mimicry of the pornographic, feminists might well feel that they should be out fly-posting this well-established dominatrix pornography, rather than trying to eliminate it. A host of empirical inquiries, from the Netherlands, Sweden, Denmark or the USA, have all failed to find any consistent correlation between the availability of pornography and sex crimes against women, many indeed have found negative correlations (not that this tells us anything about causality either). Overall, the main finding from the avalanche of correlational studies carried out over the last 20 years is that they are inconsistent, both with each other and with the claims of anti-pornography texts.

Nevertheless, it was anti-pornography campaigners, rather than their critics, who had most success in shifting the legal debate in favour of censorship during the 1990s. They boosted their appeal by joining forces with others campaigning against the less contentious injuries of 'Hate Speech' now flourishing in the USA, a move documented by Mari Matsuda and others in the 1993 *Words that Wound*. It is over a decade since MacKinnon and Dworkin first drafted their Model Ordinance, arguing that women can assert their civil rights and become fully human *only* once they win the battle against pornography. The Ordinance classifies pornography as sex discrimination ('the graphic sexually explicit subordination of women through pictures or words') and urges those who have suffered 'harm' from it to seek damages through the courts from its makers, sellers and distributors – public or private (MacKinnon 1987). After initial success in Minneapolis, the Ordinance was eventually defeated in various states of the USA following prolonged legal battles, but in Canada anti-pornography feminists (assisted by MacKinnon) were victorious, with the adoption of a modified version of the Ordinance in the Butler Supreme Court decision in 1992.

Other feminists, who have – often reluctantly – felt compelled to fight the Ordinance, in and outside the courts, argue that the relentless pursuit of such legislative change is dangerous. It relies upon vague and ambiguous terms which are certain to backfire against the sexually powerless it supposedly protects. Their fears have been realised, at least according to those who have been monitoring the effects of the Canadian legislation. Since the Butler decision, straight mainstream pornography is flourishing. Representations of alternative sexualities, by contrast, are facing increasingly intense censorship according to a study made by Brenda Cossman *et al, Bad Attitudes on Trial: Pornography Feminism and the Butler Decision.* The misappropriation of this new Canadian law, not against many men's cosily familiar sexist pornography, but rather against the more unsettling productions of sexual minorites which might work to subvert them, has been the precise and predictable outcome.

In the area of race, similar predictable reversals have occurred. The speech of the powerful remains protected (as before), the speech of minorities gets censored. Thus it is the performances of black rap groups, 2 Live Crew and Salt 'n' Pepa which have recently been targeted for censorship in US courts. As others have noticed, this strengthens the racism of conservative critics, such as Stephen Macedo, who has declared that 'rap' is the special contributon of blacks to 'American cultural degeneration'. New obscenity legislation can be a dangerous thing in its strengthening of legal powers to discriminate against the productions of unpopular cultural minorities. This is why feminists opposed to anti-pornography legislation argue that it threatens to close down spaces which women are still trying to open up in exploring how to represent themselves as sexual agents. From this perspective, the last thing we want to do is to fix the meanings of words and images independently from seeking to understand their social context and audiences. ❏

Lynne Segal is *Anniversary Professor of Psychology and Gender Studies at Birkbeck College, University of London. Her books include:* Is the Future Female? Troubled Thoughts on Contemporary Feminism; Slow Motion: Changing Masculinities, Changing Men; Sex Exposed: Feminism & the Pornography Debate, *ed. with Mary McIntosh;* Straight Sex: The Politics of Pleasure; Why Feminism? Psychology, Gender, Politics *(Polity)*

JUDITH LEVINE

The dumb-luck club

The terrorist tactics of the US pro-lifers have all but silenced the voice of those arguing for choice. The exercise of the right to abortion on demand is as rare now as it was almost half a century ago, before it was legalised

Since *Roe v Wade*, the 1973 Supreme Court decision that legalised abortion in the USA, the anti-abortion movement has been a steady presence under the dome of every legislature in the country, at every PTA meeting and on the sidewalk of every clinic. The anti-choice forces have figured in nearly every legislative change relating to youthful sex since the 1980s; and nearly every one of those new statutes moved in a restrictive direction.

The anti-abortion forces have not succeeded in their ultimate goals. Studies in the 1990s showed that the majority of girls throughout the world had sex in their teens and, while abortion rates dropped, in part because of increased use of condoms to prevent HIV transmission, US teens still got abortions at almost the rate they did when *Roe* was decided. But abortions became far harder to procure, especially if you were a kid without money or transport. By the late 1990s, there were no abortion providers in nearly one-third of the nation's metropolitan areas and 85% of US counties, according to the National Abortion Rights Action League (NARAL).

And while young women's right and ability to end a pregnancy declined, their parents' prerogative to stop them increased. As of 1999, parental notification or consent laws were in effect in 40 states. Some states forbade any unrelated person, whether a close friend, trusted minister or even a relative who was not legally the young woman's guardian, to help a girl get an abortion. A Pennsylvania woman was convicted in 1996 of 'interfering with the custody of a minor' when she drove the 13-year-old girlfriend of her 19-year-old son to a clinic in

New York state, where there are no parental consent rules. (The young man was convicted of statutory rape in the consensual relationship.) Similar legislation was proposed in Congress.

But considering the amount of clamour it's raised, one of the anti-choice movement's greatest triumphs is paradoxical: it has wrought a near-total public silence on abortion in any discussion of teen sex.

The Right's relentless condemnation of abortion has transformed the emotional and moral conception of abortion no less than the practicalities of getting one. At the beginning of the twenty-first century, one can hardly speak of abortion without a note of deep misgiving or regret – if one speaks of it at all. 'Abortion on demand and without apology', a feminist demand before *Roe* and a reality in many countries, was as rare in the USA in 1999 as it was in 1959. What this has meant for unmarried teens is that unwanted pregnancy has regained its age-old resonance of sin and doom, with motherhood once more the near-inevitable price of sexual pleasure.

While polls show that support of choice has not significantly waned, that support has become more qualified and, a quarter-century after *Roe*, the grassroots pro-choice movement is all but moribund. A splashy Feminist Expo for Women's Empowerment sponsored by the Feminist Majority Foundation in the mid-1990s could find no room for a speech or panel about women's right to choose. In an influential article in the *New Republic* in 1995, 'power feminist' Naomi Wolf scolded middle-class women for those putatively blithe 'suburban country-club rite-of-passage abortions; the "I don't know what came over me, it was such good Chardonnay" abortions' and extolled feminists to reconsider abortion within the 'paradigm of sin and redemption'. At clinics in Texas, where right-to-lifers held prayer vigils almost daily, journalist Debbie Nathan observed besieged front-line workers succumbing to a kind of Stockholm syndrome, adopting their captors' doubts as to whether abortion was such a great idea after all.

The Australian pro-choice activist Marge Ripper called this new tone the 'awfulisation of abortion'. Espousing the arguments of their antagonists, abortion's proponents became its apologists. Abortion was an evil, though a 'necessary evil,' they said. It was a deeply private 'family' affair. And it was never preferable to contraception. As the journalist Janet Hadley commented, this last argument implied, incorrectly, that contraception was always reliable and 'safe'. This made contraception the 'responsible' option – and abortion 'irresponsible.'

By the 1990s, lawyers were still fighting the restrictions in court, doctors were taking the bullets. But few pro-choicers seemed willing to defend the ethical pro-abortion position – as complex as any serious ethical position – that women's right to abortion is a moral good. Few would argue that women's right to control their fertility, to compensate for the female biological handicap of having a uterus, amounts to full existential equality of the genders; and that the use of one's body against one's will amounts to nothing less than slavery. The only moral argument for choice was made on behalf of children – that wanted children fare better in a world than hungry, neglected and abused kids.

Liberal Hollywood sure wasn't defending choice. Pregnancy panics had long been melodramatic staples for their obvious tear-jerking potential and so, for dramatic resolution purposes, were false alarms and miscarriages. But if a pregnancy lasted on screen, abortion was never an option and always a tragedy, always mourned and never forgotten. Indeed, the A-word was rarely even uttered.

These tragic narratives enact a psychological 'syndrome' invented in the late 1970s by anti-abortion 'scientists': 'post-abortion syndrome', a condition of lasting guilt, regret and physical damage allegedly caused by abortion. PAS was proved non-existent. When nearly 5,300 women, about half of whom had had abortions, were administered annual questionnaires over eight years, their levels of emotional well-being were found to be unchanged by the procedure. Claimed links between abortion and breast cancer were discovered to be similarly unfounded.

But the idea that abortion was inevitably awful took hold, particularly among teenage girls too young to have experienced the panic and peril of an unwanted pregnancy before *Roe* (or, in many cases, after it) and moved by the high melodrama and black-and-white morality of the anti-abortion script. A 14-year-old black Brooklyn teenager who miscarried told me, 'I never would have an abortion, because I'd be thinking about that baby the rest of my life.' A pregnant 16-year-old in El Paso, a wealthy white girl who was a star runner and honours student (and whose maid was going to take care of the child), was having a baby for the same reason. 'My mom wanted me to [have an abortion],' she told me. 'But oh, I couldn't live with that. Every year I'd be wondering, like, my baby would be this many years old and what would he be like?'

The little quantitative research on the subject suggested that these girls' feelings were widespread. In the early 1990s, Rebecca Stone and Cynthia Waszak ran focus groups on abortion with 13- to 19-year-olds. On the whole, the youngsters expressed 'erroneous and anecdotal evidence about abortion more often than sound knowledge, portraying the procedure as medically dangerous, emotionally damaging and widely illegal'. The source of this information, said the researchers, was largely anti-abortion propaganda, which was abundant and often targeted expressly at suggestible teens. Pro-choice opinions, on the other hand, were less widely propagated and less likely to be pointed directly at teens. In 1998, concerned about this imbalance, the Pro-Choice Education Project surveyed 16- to 24-year-old women nationwide with an eye towards designing a pro-choice public-service advertising campaign. PEP found that while almost two-thirds of their respondents selected 'pro-choice' when given the options of 'pro-choice' and 'pro-life', support was halved when the women were asked if they were 'pro-abortion'. 'They're for women's rights,' said spokesperson Marion Sullivan, 'but not necessarily for abortion.'

Young men are also affected by anti-abortion rhetoric, which, when pitched to them, plays on their attachment to male privilege. A significant minority of Canadian and US young men – about one-third – told researchers that they believed a father should have a legal prerogative to prevent a partner from having an abortion.

If kids are learning about abortion in school at all, they're learning that it is a bad thing. A 1995 survey of state laws conducted by NARAL found that only nine states specifically named abortion in their sex ed statutes. Of these, only Vermont requires that students be given neutral information; the others either forbade teachers to talk about abortion as a reproductive health method or allowed them to discuss only its negative consequences. In the one-quarter of US school districts that the Christian abstinence-promoting curriculum Sex Respect purportedly reaches, kids learn that abortion means 'killing the baby' and that its risks include 'guilt, depression, anxiety', as well as 'heavy blood loss, infection, and puncturing of the uterus'. In fact, the risks after *Roe* plummeted to 0.3 deaths per 100,000 abortions. In 1990, termination carried one-eleventh of the risk of childbirth and half the risk of a tonsillectomy.

At the time of writing, you could barely find the word abortion in the pages of 'comprehensive' sex ed curricula, either. The Girls Clubs of America's Taking Care of Business, for 'young women ages 15-18', recommended using birth control, but did not discuss the medical solution if the condom breaks or the diaphragm fails. Planned Parenthood's New Positive Images, written by a dedicated advocate of adolescents' reproductive rights, named every contraceptive method, including the morning-after pill, but left out the word abortion. Programmes for boys, finally understood as the missing link in sexual responsibility, often instructed kids in contraception, too, but especially in those aimed at inner-city youth, zoomed right past abortion to put the emphasis on marriage and fatherhood. With cosy names like 'Dads Make a Difference', these programmes transmitted the warning: if you're going to have sex, get ready to support a baby. By the 1990s, when 'abstinence' dominated the sex ed discourse, comprehensive sex educators were engaged in a contest to be best at preventing teen sex, not unwanted pregnancies or unwanted children. In such an atmosphere, a call for abortion rights was almost an admission of defeat.

Without abortion, the narrative of teenage desire was strangely, artificially unmoored from modern social reality. Instead of sound policy, the anti-abortion movement rewrote a pre-modern parable in which fate tumbles to worse fate, sin is chastised and sex is the ruination of mother, child and society. In that tale, gone was premeditation in sex, gone the role of safe contraception or 'planned parenthood'. Gone, too, was the relief, even joy, of ending an unwanted pregnancy – and women's newfound power to decide what they wanted to do with their bodies and their lives and when they wanted to do it. And in the 1990s, hideous proof became visible. Desperate girls, including middle-class high-schoolers with every opportunity before them, hid their pregnancies, gave birth in hotel rooms, stuffed their half-dead newborns into closets and trash cans. For these young women, 'getting caught', both as sexual beings and as dumb-luck mothers, was still fraught with shame and denial. Abortion had moved beyond the pale – a tragedy or a terrible secret, worse than any imaginable fate. For them there were no reproductive 'options' at all. ❏

Judith Levine *is a journalist, author, feminist and free-speech activist who lives in New York and Vermont, USA. This article in an excerpt from the forthcoming* Harmful to Minors: How sexual protectionism hurts children. *She is also the author of* My Enemy, My Love: Women, Men and the Dilemmas of Gender *(Anchor, 1993)*

defining

'I am reminded of a story that a former chief censor of Australia was fond of telling about what constituted pornography. On his classification board of ten people was a Victorian cattle farmer who sat though hundreds of sex-filled films over his first three months in the job without appearing to blink. In the fourth month, he stormed out of a screening saying he could watch most things but when it came to the 'extreme pornography' of this particular video, he drew the line. When the censor watched the film to make an independent evaluation he found that what had sent the amiable farmer off the deep end was two people having sex in gumboots!'
Robbie Swann, Eros Foundation 👁

'Pornography is a mode of representation intended or consumed for the purposes of sexual arousal.'
Mandy Merck, media arts department, Royal Holloway College, University of London, quoting the Williams Report 👁

'Porn acts as a safety valve, is useful in sex therapy and is educational. Banning porn is an insult to sex.'
Tuppy Owens, editor of the Sexual Freedom Coalition's Consenting Adults 👁

'Pornography is material designed to arouse and has no legal or consistent definition. Each person's definition depends on her upbringing, sexual preferences and viewing context.'
Feminists For Free Expression 👁

'A system of dominance and submission, pornography has the weight and significance of any other historically real torture or punishment of a group of people because of a condition of birth.'
Life and Death, *Andrea Dworkin* (Virago,1997) 👁

'Pornography is "women being treated as mere sex objects, daughters with a loss of innocence, children abused and men and women who feel trapped. Photographs, videos, magazines and virtual games that depict rape and the dehumanisation of females in sexual scenes constitute powerful but deforming tools of sex education" '
Victims of Pornography 👁

Pornography is a political practice.Obscenity is abstract; pornography is concrete. Obscenity conveys moral condemnation. Pornography identifies a political practise that is predicated on power and powerlessness- a practice that

is, in fact, legally protected.
Catherine A MacKinnon 👁

'Material that only encourages people to see one another as objects and promotes the breaking of the commandment "Thou shalt not commit adultery". Internet pornography is harmful and/or dangerous to children and the public ... and only feeds the desire of sexual offenders.'
Christians against Internet Porngography 👁

The R18 category is 'a special and legally restricted classification for videos where the focus is mainly on real sexual activity and the purpose is primarily to induce sexual arousal. Erections may be shown, as may a broader range of mild fetish material, but no threats or humiliation or realistic depictions of pain are permitted. There must be no clear sight of penetration, oral, vaginal or anal, or of masturbation. Ejaculation must not be shown.'
The British Board of Film Classification 👁

'The word pornography derives from a Greek word meaning writing about prostitutes. Although there is no widely accepted modern definition, the common element in all definitions is that the material is sexually explicit. Sexist, sexually explicit material is more a symptom than a cause of female subordination and sexual violence. Few sexual scientists judge the evidence as warranting additional restrictions.'
The Society for the Scientific Study of Sexuality, Iowa 👁

'We use the definition of the 1986 Attorney General Commission on Pornography: Material that is "predominantly sexually explicit and intended primarily for the purpose of sexual arousal". Pornography encompasses books, magazines, videos and devices and has moved from the periphery of society into the mainstream through video, soft-porn magazines and cable television.'
Leadership U, an online 'one-stop shopping superstore in the marketplace of ideas', whose mission 'is to provide answers to many of science's, religion's and life's weightier issues, free of charge'. They are sponsored by Christian Leadership Ministries 👁

Sexual objectification is another common characteristic of pornography. It refers to the portrayal of human beings-usually women- as depersonalised sexual things such as 'tits, cunts, and ass,' not as multi-faceted human beings deserving equal rights with men.
Diana E Russell. 👁

Compiled by Natasha Schmidt

MARYAM AZAD

Sisters of darkness

The wearing of the veil – *hejab* – and its enforcement since the establishment of the Islamic Republic in 1979 depends on the female agents of the regime

For the newly established Islamic Republic, the issue of *hejab* (veiling) and the public segregation of women posed a serious challenge. While the subject is rarely raised in public, even by its fiercest critics, the obsession of the among Iran's 'hardline' Muslim clerics with female dress code has remained intact for 20 years.

While they have by no means achieved their end – the complete veiling and segregation of all women – and Iranian women have continued to defy them with extraordinary inventiveness, the wearing of the *hejab* remains crucial to the identity of the regime: nothing better symbolises the Islamic Republic to the outside world than its women concealed behind their *chador* – the long black garment that represents the ultimate in Islamic 'correctness'.

The imposition of the *hejab* has always involved coercion; more important, its success depended on the complicity of women themselves. The clergy created a network of 'women agents' to assist their gangs of male thugs in enforcing *hejab* throughout the country. For millions of Iranians who witnessed the violent eruption of these *Hezbollahi* (the partisans of God), both male and female, in the later months of 1979, it was a dark moment in the progress of the Revolution. I was present when they broke up a peaceful demonstration in Tehran one afternoon in 1979, the women in their black *chador*, every bit as brutal as their male counterparts, chanting the slogan, 'Death to the unveiled.' Who were these women, where did they come from? Who did they represent? We

were told they represented the urban under class – poor prostitutes, lower-class Muslim fanatics, the marginalised residents of south Tehran's poverty-stricken slums. The reality was far more sophisticated.

The *Hezbollahi* worked under the instructions of the more extreme clerics who rapidly took over key ministries and public bodies, such as the Islamic associations that were set up immediately after the Revolution in practically every institution – factories, schools, universities, public and private companies, offices, hospitals, etc. Supported by the *komiteh* (area watch committees), each headed by a pro-Khomeini cleric, and the *Pasdaran* (Revolutionary Guards), they worked as vigilantes, organising pressure groups and their own web of informers to check and report on women who infringed the dress code.

One of the first women's vigilante groups to emerge after the Revolution was the *Basij-e-Khaharan* (Sisters of God) with its separate social and military wings. Its social wing is said to number around two million members; the size of its military wing is a closely guarded secret. The latter are involved in preliminary weapons training, conducting military manoeuvres, setting up sports and cultural camps and running courses for ideological, political and literacy training around the country. Other women's organisations, such as 'Zeynab's Sisters', have similar objectives ranging from promoting the regime's propaganda to manipulating, intimidating and controlling women in public. In Tehran, a group know as the *Gasht-e-sarallah* (Friends of God) includes women who, in association with the *Pasdaran*, arrest and detain young girls who do not observe the dress code, sometimes for as long as two days. Many groups act as indirect instruments of the regime controlling the social, cultural, public and political activities of women; others work directly for *Ershad* (Ministry of Islamic Culture and Guidance), or for *Harasat* (State Intelligence Service), identified in people's minds with the pre-revolutionary SAVAK.

Compared with the 1980s and early 1990s, the machinery of terror used to enforce the cultural aspects of the Revolution has lost some of its vigour. This is noticeable in the less rigid public segregation of women and enforcement of *hejab*. The overwhelming victory of the moderates led by Mohamed Khatami in the 1997 presidential election has been instrumental in raising women's public esteem. At a time when it is trying to distance itself from the Islamic excesses of Afghanistan's Taliban, protests by the international community and human rights

campaigners have also put pressure on the Islamic Republic to change its treatment of women in public. But the main agent of change is the women themselves, who continue to defy the regime and risk the consequences.

Many women have discovered the unpredictable nature of their tormentors: they can be everywhere and nowhere and the punishments inflicted completely arbitrary. The sisters lurk at border customs posts, in the entrances to public buildings, in shopping centres, parks, cinemas and exhibitions. At times they may offer the defiant woman a pair of stockings to cover her legs, or nail-varnish remover and tissues to wipe her nails and lipsticks; at others, punishments for precisely the same offences can include flogging.

Even the mountains to the north of Tehran, a haven for millions of the overcrowded city's inhabitants, particularly for young people denied the pleasure of consorting together in public, are not secure from the prying eyes of the sisters. 'Can you imagine,' complained Mitra, a woman out walking with a friend when a young girl was being arrested for some oinfringement of the code, 'how distressing life can be for a woman in this country? At best you are treated like a child, told what to do, how to look and what to wear. You can be intimidated, detained or even flogged simply for not observing strict *hejab*, for a few streaks of hair that have escaped from your scarf, for walking and talking with a man. If you resist this constant assault you are condemned. And do you think women would have tolerated these insults if it were not for the humiliating and inhuman consequences that might follow? Still, the regime has not succeeded. It cannot win. Its agents have to chase us everywhere, even on top of the mountains – and still we find ways of defying them.'

The sisters are paid for their work; in addition, perhaps, there is pleasure in this rare exercise of power, even if it is over other women. Over the years, these 'Angels of Darkness' have played an important role in helping the Islamic Republic institutionalise male domination and rob women of their fundamental human rights. For thousands of us who find the agents of our repression among ourselves, among those whose emancipation we seek, it is a bitter blow. ❏

Maryam Azad lives and works as a translator and interpreter in London. She visits Iran frequently

Iranian women at Kish Island – Credit: Sina/Rex

SHADAFARIN GHADIRIAN

Suspended in time

As an image, a photograph stands on its own. Rarely can such images be taken at face value. This is particularly true of studio portraits where the photographer has chosen to *construct* an image. Why construct such an image? The photographer has left clues.

The photographs here are the works of Shadi Ghadirian, a recent graduate of the Art School of Azad University in Tehran. Chosen from among her peers, the models pose with modern props in Iranian dress and against backgrounds from a century earlier. The images appear to depict a conscious choice on the part of the women.

Though a photograph should speak for itself, one cannot be oblivious to the fact that what we see are constructed images of her own gender, at a particular moment in history, created by a young Iranian woman. As opposed to the work of a few women photographers from the Middle East, living and exhibiting in the West, that explores the notion of the 'western image of eastern woman' and their personal alienation, Ghadirian's photographs are unique. They are images from within that do not play on western sensitivities but stand on their own. ❏

From the introduction to **Shadafarin Ghadirian***'s London exhibition in February this year, written by* **Reza Sheikh**

Female genital mutilation

KOLPOKA, NORTH-EAST GHANA

'You see, I was brought up to see FGM as a positive thing, my initiation into womanhood. One man held me down across my chest and four others held my legs and arms. Using a knife, the circumcisor removed my clitoris, cleared the inside of my vagina and left it plain. I was made to do a vigorous dance to show that I was a brave girl and happy about the operation. I got infected and there was a 'growth' where my clitoris had been. I had to be cut again twice to remove it. Afterwards I had no feelings towards men at all. It took me a very long time to get pregnant – about six years. You see, I have never enjoyed sex because it was always so painful. When I got pregnant for the first time I had such a very difficult labour. The scar tissue made it so hard for the baby. The child did not survive. I am 35 now and I have three children, twin boys and a girl. I have suffered much and wouldn't dream of even whispering the existence of this practice to my daughter.'

FADUME'S STORY

'I was so excited. It was such a big day for me. I was the centre of attention and everyone was so happy for me. I felt so special. I was looking forward to all the presents. I would have a new dress and my first pair of shoes. My mother said I would bring honour to my family today … I felt so proud…

'I remember when I saw the knife, I wanted to run, but I couldn't move. There were three women holding me down. I tried to be strong, but when they started to cut me I screamed, it hurt so much. I lost consciousness and I don't remember anything else until it was finished. I had to stay in bed with my legs tied together for almost two weeks. It still hurt terribly and I cried and cried. I bled a lot and was weak for many months.'

FGM has no firm foundation in any religion.

FGM is usually performed with unsterilised knives, razors or glass and without anaesthesia. It us makes intercourse – and often childbirth – exceedingly painful, and is practised by male-domin societies to keep wives faithful and young girls virgins.

FGM is practised in more than 20 sub-Saharan countries, as well as among some religious sec Malaysia, India, Pakistan, Oman, South Yemen and the UAE.

Immigration has imported FGM into Europe, the USA and Australia, although it contravenes UNIC Convention on the Rights of the Child and is illegal in these countries.

Parents immigrating to the US from countries that perform the ritual are warned they face up to years in prison if they arrange for their daughters to be genitally mutilated in the US.

US Centers for Disease Control estimate that more than 150,000 women and girls of African c living in the US have been or are at risk of being genitally mutilated.

There have been five cases of FGM among pregnant immigrant women in the San Jose area of Calif since 1980. This has prompted the introduction of a bill outlawing FGM in California.

The US Immigration and Naturalization Service says it will argue in court that female genital mutilati adequate grounds for asylum after Fauziya Kasinga, 20, from Togo, was told by a Philadelphia judge that her story of FGM was unbelievable and was insufficient grounds for being granted political asylum.

In France in 1982, a three-month-old girl died as the result of an excision performed by a traditional excisor. Her parents were charged with criminal negligence and given suspended sentences.

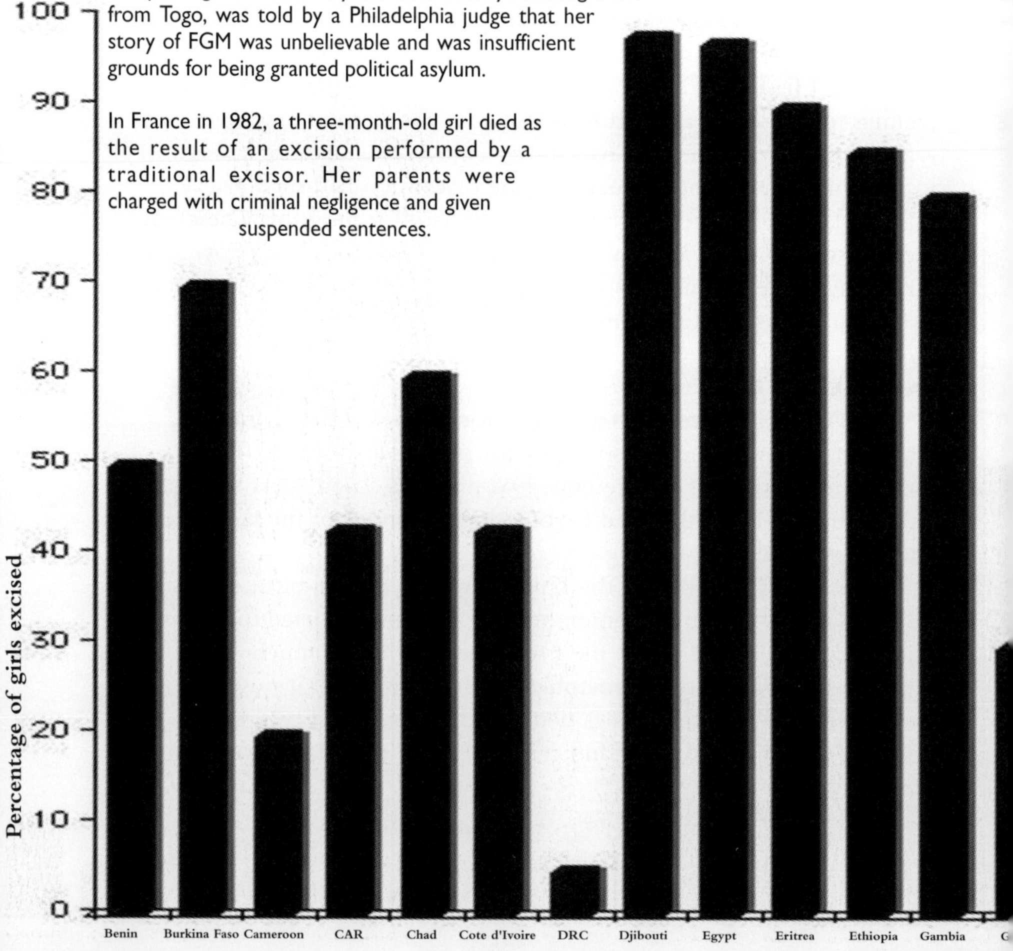

Bar chart — Percentage of girls excised, by country: Benin ~50, Burkina Faso ~70, Cameroon ~20, CAR ~42, Chad ~59, Cote d'Ivoire ~42, DRC ~5, Djibouti ~97, Egypt ~96, Eritrea ~90, Ethiopia ~85, Gambia ~79, G... ~29

he last ten to 15 years, France has criminally prosecuted parents in more than 30 families for having
ir daughters genitally mutilated.

re have been no prosecutions in Britain against practitioners of FGM.

World Health Organisation estimates that up to 130 million women and girls today, in at least 28
ntries, have had their genitals cut.

representatives to financial institutions such as the World Bank, which have lent money to
ntries where FGM is practised, will be required to oppose loans to those governments that fail to
ry out educational programmes to prevent the practice.

egalese women and men in 29 villages have banned the practice of female genital mutilation as of
e 1998.

Malian father brought his baby girl into a Paris hospital in 1982 after he 'removed her clitoris with a
cket knife'.

991, a UK survey of social services departments in Britain revealed that 'Of 65 local social work -
artments surveyed, ten reported casework intervention because of suspected genital mutilation.'

rces: Womankind, UK-based women's rights campaigning organisation; *Female Genital Mutilation*, Nahid Toubia and Susan Izett
3; The Hosken's Report, Fran Hosken (1978 but figures updated to 1996); *New York Times*, *San
cisco Chronicle*; *Washington Post*; *Cutting the Rose: Female Genital Mutilation, the Practice and its
Prevention*, Efua Dorkenoo (Minority Rights
Publications 1994)

| a-Bissau | Kenya | Liberia | Mali | Mauritania | Niger | Nigeria | Senegal | Sierra Leone | Somalia | Sudan | Togo | Uganda | Tanzania |

IRENA MARYNIAK

Something to think about

With the disintegration of the socialist system throughout eastern Europe, wife beating is on the increase. But everyone conspires to keep the secret: women are ashamed to report it; and if they do, the authorities dismiss it as trivial

Ildi had arrived at the Feny haza shelter in Budapest two days before and she wasn't sure if she really had anything worth telling. 'It's so banal,' she said. Her husband was a Reformed Church pastor. They had recently been living in a Hungarian village just north of the Croatian border. There were no jobs. The men moped in a dingy little *bierkeller*, the women worried about the kids. At home, in the medieval university town of Pecs, Ildi had trained as a teacher of French and computer studies. Here, she was lonely. The villagers were polite but distant. Her husband preached. Then he drank. He wouldn't let her see her old friends. He got violent. 'I couldn't help him,' she said. 'He beat me regularly; and the children. He'd lock us in the attic. He'd punch me in the jaw and ram his fist into the back of my neck. He kicked me. He tried to strangle me. He cut my eye with a bottle. You can see the scar. He told me I was Satan. Then one night he battered my son while he was asleep and made him kneel on the floor until dawn. That was when I thought, enough.' Ildi took her children and fled to Budapest. Her husband continues to preach.

Evidence suggests that the culture of giving the wife something to think about crosses every boundary: cultural, social, economic, racial, religious, regional. Worldwide, an estimated 60 million women are missing from population statistics – they should be alive and they're not. In parts of eastern Europe, where the rate of recorded homicide has doubled in the past decade, about half of killings happen in the home. Every week, a Hungarian woman dies in a domestic argument and violence is estimated to feature in at least half of all long-term relationships. In Russia, 14,000 women a year are killed by their partners and 57,000 battered. In Poland, over 60% of divorced women say they were beaten. Not everyone tells, of course, and information is fragmentary: what estimates there are come from surveys conducted by the few women's groups in central and eastern Europe and, recently, by UNICEF (*Women in Transition*, Regional Monitoring report, No 6, 1999). The victims themselves are overwhelmingly silent.

In former communist countries, women were once herded into collective farms and factories and exhorted to be heroine mothers at the same time. The political transition displaced most of them from their jobs in the early 1990s and planted them squarely back home. The chance to shed part of the multiple load of manual work, child-bearing, queuing, cooking, cleaning, feeding and loving doubtless came as a welcome relief to many. But in an environment of increasing insecurity and income inequality, where violence is never far from the surface, women now bear the brunt of family trauma and hardship. In eastern and central Europe, they have become as vulnerable to assault at home as they have to sexual exploitation in the new labour market.

Under old totalitarian regimes, a two-room flat was the stronghold where individuality was nurtured, expressed and guarded: the 'life prize', as Slavenka Drakulic has written, 'which set the border between private and public'. It marked the boundary between civil societies in embryo, and state power. There, in cramped kitchens, debate about politics and culture was possible. Outside it was not. Home was the forum for 'anti-politics', the dissident practice of behaving as if one lived in a democratic polity, a private civil society. This was where people wrote and published their *samizdat*, held seminars and launched small businesses. It was the autonomous space, and within it mistresses, wives and daughters were expected to provide the emotional, practical and often material sustenance for the intellectual and political activities of their men. Their function was to maintain the private realm for the practice of dissent.

In the new democracies, the private haven, the family, has been declared all but sacrosanct. It mustn't be defiled by the community. Public discourse dominated by nationalist sentiment is encouraging women to think in terms of procreating for the nation. At home, they

ានអំពើហិង្សា នាំឲ្យគ្រួសារវិនាស

បញ្ឈប់ការវាយដំទៀតទៅ

Phnom Penh, anti-domestic violence poster –
Credit: Sean Sprague/Panos

are the ones who will establish new mores, consolidate national identity, and create the foundations for lasting self-determination. The Soviet image of the hero-mother has been replaced by the icon of the national-mother, a designer-clad Holy Virgin, whose home – cosy, cute and, preferably, suburban – is the domain of natural order. Crimes don't happen there.

In some parts of the former communist world – Armenia, Georgia, Bulgaria – beating up your partner at home isn't a criminal offence. In Slovenia, it is not a crime in cases of light injuries like 'a fractured nose, rib, light contusions and punched-out teeth'. Eight countries in the region do not consider marital rape a crime. In Hungary, nine out of ten people think abuse in the family is a private matter. The police won't interfere unless there really is blood on the parquet. Evidence is reluctantly collected and treated with suspicion; neighbours won't get involved. 'A lot of people batter their women,' Ildi says. 'Older women tell you to be patient. You have to hold on.' Violence is part of daily life: the woman was provocative, she spoke, she misbehaved, she upset the shape of things, she had to be brought to heel.

Professionals in health, policing, the judiciary and social services are untrained in dealing with cases of domestic abuse and treat them as trivial incidents. In Poland, numerous medical certificates are needed for a case to be taken to court. They cost over US$10 each, which is usually prohibitive, and the woman has to pay. Investigations are intimidating and embarrassing and there is no protection from retaliation by the defendant. There are very few shelters. In 90% of cases, conviction means a suspended sentence for the batterer. Most of those imprisoned get a one-year sentence. In Russia, general prosecutors reportedly like to remark that if women obeyed their husbands there would be fewer beatings. Police often refuse complaints. There is a widespread assumption that rape in marriage is impossible and most women have no idea where to seek help.

Reporting of rape is down everywhere; estimates reckon it is five to ten times higher than reported (up to 30 times higher in Poland). The popular belief in Hungary is that rape without consent simply doesn't happen. 'You can't put a thread in a moving needle', the Hungarian saying goes. Women prefer to keep their heads down rather than expose themselves to the embarrassment, humiliation and stigma of turning to the authorities.

Feny haza is the only shelter in Budapest exclusively for battered women and their children. One woman reported recently that she had watched her partner sexually abuse her two daughters for months, living in a one-room flat with a mezzanine to which she was relegated under threat of beating every night. She had been to the police of course. There she had been told that to proceed with the case would only get her into deeper trouble. After all, she had allowed it to happen. 'It's most likely just a ploy to get her hands on the apartment,' a police officer remarked.

There is nowhere to go. The housing shortage, women's lack of economic independence, the fact that many couples have to live together during and after divorce, that there is no such thing as a restriction order and that it is up to the woman to get out – all these contribute to the blanket of silence over domestic abuse. If the woman does leave home she forfeits the right to any share of the property when she divorces. And then there is the disapproval, the shame, the nagging emotional dependence, the loss of self-esteem, the fear. To resist, to speak and show signs of breaking out are the most dangerous things she can do. That is when killings happen.

The endurance of so many east European women is a reflection of their mistrust of the authorities, the weakness of their position in law, their fragile sense of personal dignity and anxiety for themselves and their children. Publicly, their plight is trivialised and, as far as possible, ignored, although extreme cases of sexual violence get all the hype you'd expect, particularly if paedophilia features. The perpetrator is likely to be presented as a psychopathic alien: evil and foreign. Because the danger is out there, not here, at home, in the home.

The one book on domestic abuse that had appeared in Hungary, Krisztina Morvai's *Terror in the Family*, prompted a leading criminal lawyer to say on television that the book was so popular he rather wished he was a battered woman himself. Morvai survived attempts to rubbish her as a third-rate academic driven by unspeakable experiences, and has remained hugely in demand. Writing the book was empowering for the women she interviewed, she says. 'They saw it become a public issue, part of public discourse. Not that this necessarily helps them. It's up to the law to stop it. Legislation should lead the way. It's as though the male world doesn't want to see the issue in a broader framework. We don't want to associate battering with white middle-class culture. If a white man becomes a batterer it's a matter of individual psychology. If he's from a minority, like the Roma community, it becomes cultural.'

'I want to go away ... so there'll be no such conflicts,' Kati says, very quietly. She is Roma, and her partner started beating her after she spent three months in hospital following the birth of her third child who was severely handicapped. She left because he threatened her mother. 'I don't believe it's possible to have a good relationship,' she murmurs. 'Sooner or later the problem will return. I'd like a secure life in which no one will come and break down the door, where I don't need to depend on a man, materially or in other ways. There are people out there who live like that. I believe I could too.'

Out there are disintegrating social and health services, minimal social benefits and jobs demanding personal extras. There is sexual harassment, stalking, a vulnerable labour market. There is prostitution (many Russian women think of it as a euphemism for freedom), there is trafficking, international crime, a mafia-style culture. There are ads for women 'without inhibitions' and for 'blonde' office managers 'with long legs'. And, just below the surface, there is coercion and violence.

Since 1917, the heartlands and plains of central and eastern Europe have seen two world wars, revolution and civil strife, the Holocaust, decades of totalitarian rule and, most recently, ethnic cleansing in which rape and forced pregnancy were used as weapons of war. Despite a veneer of sometimes ostentatious courtesy, personal dignity is a long way down the list of real social priorities. Everyone remembers what lies under the surface. Everyone knows what it is to be hit – children, pupils, conscripts, mental patients, suspects in police custody. Brutality is real, not virtual.

In Croatia, firearms distributed during the war haven't all been recovered and are alleged to have been used in homes against women and children. During the war in Yugoslavia between 1993 and 1995, 40% of callers to the SOS Belgrade hotline for women said they had been threatened with weapons. At about the same time, there was a case in Hungary of a man who held a nine-year-old girl at knife-point for a whole afternoon, after her mother had walked out on him. Finally, when he realised his former partner had persuaded the police to take notice, he hacked her daughter to death. 'It'll be a lesson to the bitch,' he remarked later to witnesses. He was found to be medically sound of mind and everyone was baffled. ❏

Irena Maryniak

YASMIN ALIBHAI-BROWN

Smother love

**Fear, confusion and mutual incomprehension combine to
perpetuate the abuse of Asian women in the UK**

Zoora Shah, a middle-aged woman who poisoned her lover after
allegedly suffering abuse at his hands, is still in prison in spite of
campaigns to release her. The trial judge did not believe she couldn't tell
anyone of her abuse. Like most other white Britons, he did not
understand the dynamics, values and factors that underpin the lives of
British Asian women.

This case is an acting-out of the tensions between different traditions,
the realities of immigration and the complexities that arise in
multicultural societies. It is about the fundamental values of this country
and the changing lives and core beliefs of minority groups, which cannot
be explained simply in terms of patriarchy and victim women. I talked
to Asian women about the Shah case. Most of them despised her and
thought she should have killed herself before bringing this shame on the
community. Since her conviction, there have been several other cases
showing how women are implicated in the serious abuse of young
women in their families for not showing due obedience. Mothers and
mothers-in-law kill their own and show no regret. When accused they
cry 'culture' or say that they acted not out of choice but responsibility.
The deep reality of these statements needs to be better understood.

All our myths, religious texts (Sita, Draupadi and Damayanti, the
symbols of perfect womanhood in the *Ramayana* are always saintly,
obedient and self-sacrificing), popular songs and films tell us that the role
of our parents is to hand us over intact and submissive into the
controlling hands of our husbands and families. Muslims and Sikhs
violate their own tenets and declare that women are never to be free
agents, ideas that once prevailed in this country too. The feminist

Madhu Kishwar, author of *Gandhi and Women*, described how Gandhi tried to change these beliefs in subtle ways by redescribing these mythical women. He rejected utterly the idea that women should be seen as 'the tools' or as slaves of men. Autonomy, fearlessness and the right to say no were non-negotiable rights he said. And yet, 50 years on, although many of us are empowered and proud to be Asian, far too many Asian women remain without even a sense of free will and, like brainwashed soldiers, many readily destroy the women who will not surrender this basic right.

In Pakistan, Samia Imram, who was seeking to leave a forced marriage, was gunned down last year in the office of her lawyers by a killer hired by her mother who is a doctor. Ruksana Ahmed was seven months pregnant when her brother strangled her while her mother held her down. It is women who insist on genital mutilation even when men oppose it. Women are the custodians of virtue and cultural continuity in these communities and they perform the role with grim determination.

Diasporic people often become more stubbornly conservative and it is the women who are always blamed if the children get rebellious. Women worry, too, that in throwing out the worst aspects of their cultures they will also surrender values they hold dear. It is important, for example, to respect the older members of the family without permitting them to own you. But change can never be kept barking on the outside and the idea of a partnership is replacing the notion of ownership in marriage. Not though, among the most deprived and easily threatened groups, such as the Mirpuris in Bolton and the rural Bangladeshis and Sikhs in other parts of the country, where there is evidence of increasing oppression. Young girls, deeply loved as children, are imprisoned, beaten, starved by the men and the older women in the family, who fear being ostracised themselves. Many girls run away from home. Some are taken on 'holiday' and forced into marriages before they finish school. Others are recaptured after their education. Mothers are always involved. In 1998, Sekina Khan and Mohammed Bashir were jailed for the unlawful kidnapping of their daughter Rehana, after spiking her drink. There is anecdotal evidence that a number of such young women have committed suicide. As the only Asian woman columnist in the mainstream press, I get calls from a huge number of distressed girls. They ask me for help I cannot give them and it breaks me up.

So do I believe that these mothers are monsters? No. Sekina, by all accounts, loves her children. She worked hard in their corner shop to get that good life, believing that the children would not be seduced by the ways of the West (stereotyped in these communities as irredeemably evil) and that they would all carry on happy ever after as if they had never left that spot in the subcontinent which is still home in their hearts. Some religious and community leaders have encouraged these responses instead of enabling parents such as Sekina, many of whom are illiterate and easily led, to manage the inevitable changes in their lives. But the children have changed, have become more individualistic and self-aware. Most have not become 'westernised' in any crude sense, but nor are they like their parents used to be. It is fear that drives these parents to cruelty and things will only change when those who determine the values of a community – the religious leaders in particular, whose instructions are rarely disobeyed even by the most brutish – can tell older women that God will punish them if they torture their daughters and daughters-in-law, and that these cultures will only survive if young girls are made to feel happy within them. ❏

Yasmin Alibhai-Brown, journalist and broadcaster, is a weekly columnist for the Independent. *She is the author of* No Place Like Home *and* True Colours. *Her new book,* Who Do We Think We Are?*(Penguin), is due out in April*

JASMINA TESANOVIC

Mothers and daughters

If women accept the construct put on them by men, that makes them the worst censors in the world

There are men who claim that women are the great censors of life: for example, the Pope. Only recently, His Holiness said the greatest crime against life last century was abortion.

Nevertheless, I'm grateful my mother didn't censor my little life but delivered me in pain and glory. Being a doctor and a communist living when and where she did, she could have had an abortion as painlessly as a tooth extraction. I also flatter myself she wanted me, her baby girl, just me and nobody else. On the contrary, when I was born my father said: 'How can I face my friends? Such a big man with a female child.' He didn't know the other Serbian proverb: only the biggest womanisers are gifted – or punished – with daughters.

If we accept the construct put on us by men – that we are no more than biological bodies without free will or selves – then women really are the biggest censors in the world.

Let me recount an incident during our most recent war in Kosovo, some time in 1998. As the latest cycle of violence burst in the south of Serbia, our president's wife opened a new maternity hospital. The ceremony was pompous; her speech long. For the entire two hours duration, every woman who arrived in labour was turned away. I always wondered what happened to them: no ceremony can stop a delivery; no power on earth can stop creation. The story of women as censors and killers as well as bearers of life begins there, in a maternity hospital.

My mother was always the main censor of my freedom, first of my life, then of my speech and self-expression. Her advice, well known and popular among Serbian women, was that women can have it all only if they know how to keep their heads down. I didn't follow it and, as a result, according to her, ruined my life. She taught me how to be quiet and keep other women quiet so that we could 'have it all' some day. I did it to my daughter in turn, but subconsciously, out of love. To have it all, as most men do, we women have to start from scratch, from silence.

Now that my mother is gone, besides a terrible freezing wind of loneliness, I also feel free; too free: free to be misunderstood, free to die, free to be bad. I can hardly survive. I am looking towards the childish face of my daughter: is she big enough to be my partner, to censor me as I did her? With the same preciseness and decision? I am lonely in this world of open male conspiracy, they don't even bother to hide the rules; on the contrary, they turn them into laws, calling them universal or just. So boring, so obvious: they don't know how to use the words and express forbidden things without actually saying them: that's poetry, and poetry belongs to all women but few men. The world of men, though not women, is that of laws and rules. No more warmth and communion of the subdued, of the humiliated and offended. We all live in soap operas, unaware of the bubbles we produce, which we call big thoughts.

Now that my mother is gone, I am like Anna Karenina, Jane Eyre, Scarlett O'Hara, Rebecca: like any uncensored or exposed woman in the literary or other public sphere. And all of us expect these women, motherless daughters or mothers of daughters, to act differently: to be better, I guess, than those inner little selves we are hiding and running away from. But there is nowhere to run, nowhere to hide: it's a big world and a bad one; far less safe, less cosy than our private domain.

When I grew up, my mother tried to protect me by taking my life away from me and living it for me: living it differently from the way she'd lived her own; keeping me beautiful and clean and happy in a vase, for ever. When I told her I was pregnant, she answered in denial: 'It's not possible, you're not married,' and then went with me to the hospital to have my baby. When I brought my baby home, she took it from me saying: 'You must be free and study to be a good mother,' and so my baby and I became sisters sharing a mother but with different fathers. But when I wanted to leave the baby and go out for a drink she would say: 'You can't go; you must be a good mother.'

It has taken me years to admit she won: despite my struggle against her, she managed to make sisters of us, slave and master of each other. I managed to separate from her but not from my daughter: We live in complicity without getting along, alternating the mother/daughter roles.

In conclusion, another anecdote. When I think of my president's wife I always think of the most powerless person in the world becoming the most powerful woman in my country. She considers herself a writer, a philosopher, a poet and inspiration of her husband, his best friend and counsellor. That is why most of his friends and enemies hate and fear her. She is a parody of Lady Macbeth – everything in my country today is a parody of something – yet a dangerous one. Not so with my president, an indicted war criminal. He loves his irrational passionate wife but, in the end, will do whatever he wants – that is to say, whatever he needs to do to stay in power – without taking his family or people into his confidence. He doesn't feel responsible to anybody but himself. She does the dirty work of explaining and justifying him. I also know that if he were to disappear, everyone would turn against her in a flash, especially women who envy her powerless power: the crown of their common position. When I listen to her speeches I hear the things men call stupid but that ring true to me, however banal or dangerous. In a speech about the New World Order she will mention her son who sends her love messages on a pager, or her thoughts on those rainy days when she cries sitting at her window. I am afraid of her, for her, for all of us.

When I think of the way she looks back at me from the TV screen, I feel uncomfortable; I feel ashamed of and for her. She shouldn't expose all that female power. And I feel like censoring her: telling her that the men who vote for her husband hate her. And I remember what my mother used to tell me about her: she's a nice woman, a true communist. But she shouldn't have gone into public life with her husband around. But that's because she didn't have a mother around to help her out with all those men in power.

The story is actually much more cruel: my president's wife was born in the woods, in 1942, during the heavy persecution of her mother, an active communist. Her father, a famous communist leader too, assisted the delivery. The baby was given away the same day to the grandparents and the mother was killed a year or so later by her own companions, as a traitor, for giving away secrets when tortured by the enemy.

I guess, even more than in a maternity hospital, everything begins and ends, as in all good fables, in the woods. ❑

Jasmina Tesanovic is a Belgrade-based writer and publisher

GORDANA IGRIC

Censor with a flower

Mirjana Markovic is not only the influential wife of Yugoslav President Slobodan Milosevic, she is Serbia's supreme censor. Most Serbs also believe she is the 'passionate ideologue' – or evil genius – behind her husband's wars

Mirjana Markovic was born on 10 July 1942, during WWII. Her mother, a leader of the partisan movement in Pozarevac, a small town near Belgrade, gave birth deep inside partisan territory. On the same day, Mirjana was taken from her mother and given to her grandmother. Soon after, her mother was arrested by the police, and died under torture. When the police started to arrest party members who had been close to her, she was posthumously sentenced for 'cowardly behaviour' and branded a traitor.

Until recently, Mirjana wore a red silk rose in her hair, an affectation copied from an old photograph of her mother. It became the symbol of her husband's party, the ruling Socialist Party of Serbia. Mirjana never accepted this 'fabrication' and grew up determined to avenge the 'careerists and intriguers' who had betrayed her mother.

For years, her father was in the top echelons of the Serbian Communist Party, close to the almighty Josep Broz Tito. Mirjana was an outsider in his new family. Summer holidays in Tito's exclusive summer resorts did no more than offer a glimpse of life among the Party elite before returning to the drab provincialism of life with her grandparents.

Serbs still remember Mirjana's rhapsodic diary in *Duga* magazine in 1993 at a time when Sarajevo was being shelled daily, rampant hyperinflation was reducing the population to poverty and every day four starving elderly people would commit suicide in Belgrade. While the citizens of former Yugoslavia – Croats, Bosnians, Albanians and finally the Serbs themselves – were losing their homes, the woman with a flower in her hair was writing about the clouds floating above the house of her birth in the town of Pozarevac and about the grasshopper who lived there. She wrote of the concern she and her son Marko shared for the winter survival of the fragile insect.

Mira's career as a censor began in the late 1980s while a professor at the university in Belgrade; it blossomed during the NATO bombardment of Serbia, with the murder of Slavko Curuvija, owner of the daily *Dnevni Telegraf* and the weekly magazine *Evropljanin*.

In the months leading up to his death, he had spearheaded a campaign for the freedom of the media in the face of government control. His papers were heavily fined, their equipment confiscated and their publication in Serbia banned. Several days before his murder, *Politika Ekspres*, a daily controlled by the Milosevics, published a piece with the headline 'Curuvija waited for the bombs'. Its author quoted Mirjana Markovic's warning to Curuvija and others who defied them: 'If they think their treason will be forgotten, they hope in vain.' He became a marked man. In her book, those who opposed the government were not only 'NATO mercenaries', they were homosexuals, sick people in failed marriages, the scum of the earth and allies of those who were murdering their own people.

In December last year, Mirjana stated it as her considered opinion that it was high time the media was 'decontaminated'. The restrictive press law passed by her party, Yugoslav United Left, in coalition with her husband's, the Socialist Party of Serbia was not enough (*Index* 6/98).

She also initiated a witch-hunt in the university, claiming that those lecturers who happened to be members of the opposition 'offered narcotics and foreign money' to their students in lieu of debate on theoretical, academic and philosophical subjects. Furthermore, she claimed, they took their money and their instructions from the foreign embassies in the capital.

The space controlled by the Milosevic couple gets ever narrower, as does the choice of enemies at whom to point her 'threatening finger'. Those who know Mirjana Markovic warn their friends: beware. ❏

Gordana Igric is a Serbian journalist working with the Institute for War and Peace Reporting

Man in the balance

'Today is 6 February 2000. I'm relatively okay. The only problem is that I can't get home right now. Well, I feel fine here – as fine as one can hope to feel when a war is going on. The people around me are trying to be helpful. The only "but" is that I'm longing to be home again, I want it all to be over at long last. Anyway, don't worry about me. I hope I'll be home soon. That's all I wanted to say.'

It was the first anyone had heard of Andrey Babitsky, Russian correspondent for *Radio Svoboda* (Liberty), since 20 January when he had telephoned his Moscow office before going to Grozny. The message came from a video the station had purchased for US$300 from 'Aleksey', a Chechen from Istanbul. Babitsky's image was blurred and he was alone and seemed ill at ease, but otherwise unharmed. Time and place where the clip was shot remain a mystery.

The government and army initially denied any knowledge of Babitsky's whereabouts, suggesting he might have been detained in Chechnya, a region notorious for the kidnapping of journalists (*Index* 1/1998). Indeed, this fear of kidnap had deterred journalists from trying to penetrate the official information blockade which, throughout the siege of Grozny, silenced anything from the front other than the thunder of the Russian guns and the wilder claims of their military spokesmen. Conditions in the 'filtration camps', where Chechen civilians are interned, the number of civilian dead in Grozny, the army's own losses, the resistance's allegedly Islamist backers: these were easily kept secrets with intimidated journalists held on such a tight leash.

Babitsky was an exception. A veteran of the earlier Chechen war (1994–1996), he had reportedly volunteered as a hostage in June 1995 when a group of fighters led by Chechen warlord Shamil Basayev killed over 100 civilians in Budenovsk, and took a further 1,000 captive. He had done little since to endear him to the military or to Rosinformcenter, the information service established by acting-President Vladimir Putin as a more efficient means of news management (*Index* 1/2000). In January, Babitsky had filed hard-hitting stories about the mutilation of Russian conscripts and the heavy casualties among the Russian inhabitants of Grozny.

Rumours about Babitsky's fate began to filter through towards the end of January. He had been arrested in or near the war zone on 16 January, according to one, and charged under Presidential Decree No. 1815: 'On measures to prevent vagabondism and beggary'. Twelve days later, the Ministry of Internal

Affairs said he had been arrested on the Grozny-Gudermes road for not having the proper accreditation. On 31 January, a presidential spokesman admitted he was being held in a filtration camp in Chernokozovo, charged with 'taking part in an illegal armed formation'. Babitsky was no better than a Chechen spy.

At a Rosinformcenter briefing three days later, presidential spokesman Sergei Yastrzhembsky told the press that, at the written suggestion of a Chechen field commander known as Turpal Ali Abgireyev, Babitsky had been exchanged for two Russian soldiers being held prisoner in Grozny. He showed a letter purporting to be Babitsky's assent to the transaction. On 4 February, Russian TV showed footage of the journalist in the process of being handed over to a masked man.

The Chechens denied any knowledge of Babitsky's whereabouts a day later, pointing out that the warlord Abgireyev had been killed days before the exchange was mooted. Doubts about the video's authenticity began to surface. The Glasnost Defence Foundation called it a 'crude fabrication', pointing out that Babitsky was released by his Russian captors into a snow-covered highway scene, while the second part of the film shows him in a roadway free of snow. Colleagues questioned the handwriting in Babitsky's supposed letter.

According to Amnesty International, the videotape had been delivered to *Radio Svoboda* by a Chechen, who arrived in a Mercedes, accompanied by a man dressed in military fatigues decorated with badges of the interior ministry's armed force, OMON. The Chechen said Babitsky was being held by Chechens in Alkhazurovo but, a day later on 7 February, a letter arrived from a conscript who claimed to have seen the journalist in Gudermes in the hands of the pro-Russian Chechen leader, Bislan Gantamirov. He wrote that his face was swollen and bruised and there was blood on his coat.

The kidnapping of Babitsky has since become symbolic of the state of Russian journalism under Putin, who has presided over the most efficient muzzling of the press since *glasnost*. On 9 February, he told the press that 'the freedom of the press is an essential element for the development of the state'; on 16 February, 30 or more newspapers collaborated in a special edition, distributed free in Moscow, on the disappearance of Babitsky. On its front page, stated: 'For the first time in years, freedom of speech is under attack ... What has happened to Andrey Babitsky ... is not an isolated event but a turning point in the fight for a press that is the servant of the people and not of government.'

Like the war itself, Putin's creeping control of the media is all part of the grand plan to ensure his victory in the March presidential election. Babitsky's life is a price he is prepared to pay. ❏

MG

A censorship chronicle incorporating information from the American Association for the Advancement of Science Human Rights Action Network (AAASHRAN), Amnesty International (AI), Article 19 (A19), the BBC Monitoring Service Summary of World Broadcasts (SWB), *the Committee to Protect Journalists (CPJ), Canadian Journalists for Free Expression (CJFE), Glasnost Defence Foundation (GDF), Instituto de Prensa y Sociedad (IPYS), The UN's Integrated Regional Information Network (IRIN), the Inter-American Press Association (IAPA), the International Federation of Journalists (IFJ/FIP), Human Rights Watch (HRW), the Media Institute of Southern Africa (MISA), Network for the Defence of Independent Media in Africa (NDIMA), International PEN (PEN), Open Media Research Institute (OMRI), Pacific Islands News Association (PINA), Radio Free Europe/Radio Liberty (RFE/RL), Reporters Sans Frontières (RSF), the World Association of Community Broadcasters (AMARC), World Association of Newspapers (WAN), the World Organisation Against Torture (OMCT) and other sources*

ANGOLA

On 10 December police forced the weekly independent *Folha 8* and *Agora* newspapers to drop their lead story, a scathing critique of the government's systematic abuse of oil revenues based on the report 'A Crude Awakening' published by the British NGO Global Witness in December. The report charges multinational oil companies BP-Amoco and Exxon/Mobil with a lack of accounting transparency and names key businessmen and

generals close to President Eduardo dos Santos whose manipulation of national oil revenues has so far escaped close scrutiny, particular by Angola's donors. (MISA)

Andre Domingos Mussamo, editor-in-chief of Angolan National Radio and correspondent for *Folha 8*, is still being detained without charge since his arrest on 2 December for 'stealing state documents and violating state secrets'. His detention, now over 70 days, well exceeds the permitted maximum. The action relates to an unpublished article written for *Folha 8* that referred to a letter written to President Dos Santos. (MISA)

On 24 December the Luanda Tribunal sentenced journalist **Gustavo Costa** to a one-year suspended sentence and a fine of 2,850 kwanzas (US$508) for 'defaming' the chief of the Civil Office of the President, José Leitao. Costa also had to pay compensation of US$20,000. The charges followed an article last April on corruption at the presidential palace *Index* 4/1999, 5/1999). (MISA)

On 19 January MP Mendes de Carvalho of the ruling MPLA issued a death threat against journalist **Rafael Marques** during a parliamentary debate on freedom of the press. De Carvalho said that if Marques continued to criticise in writing the president, he 'will not live to the age of forty'. Marques is twenty-eight. (MISA)

ARGENTINA

Argentina may become the first

Latin American country in which journalists cannot be jailed for criticising public officials, following approval on 15 December of a bill to decriminalise libel and defamation. The proposed law introduces the 'real malice' standard first articulated by the US Supreme Court in the *New York Times* v Sullivan case in 1959. Under the new rule, plaintiffs in civil libel cases would not only have to prove that the published information was false, but that the author knew or should have known it was false. (CPJ)

Security Minister of Buenos Aires province Aldo Rico allegedly insulted and threatened photographers **María Eugenia Cerruti** of *Clarín*, **Facundo Pechervsky** of *La Nación* and **Federico Guastavino** of *Noticias* magazine, accusing them of publishing 'lies and hypocrisies' during his visit to Pinamar region on 4 January. Rico apologised the following day on the order of the provincial governor. (Periodistas)

Police superintendent Daniel Del Castillo, who last April was accused of physically and verbally attacking three journalists, struck out again on 6 January against a press photographer covering the policeman's testimony in an extortion and bribery case. Del Castillo, of the Santiago del Estero police force, called journalists 'criminals' and attempted to assault the unnamed photographer. (IAPA)

Three producers and a cameraman from television station Cablevisión Sur were attacked on 19 January by employees of the municipality of Merlo, in western Buenos Aires, where they were trying to film the burning of rubbish in a local quarry. Later that day, the journalists received several threats from an anonymous caller. (IFJ)

ARMENIA

The mass-circulation daily *Haykakan Zhamanak* did not publish on 24 December after a local businessman led an attack on the paper's male staff the previous day. Reporters said Gagik Tsaroukian, accompanied by a dozen burly men, burst into their editorial offices late on 23 December to rough up editor-in-chief **Nikol Pashinian** and his colleagues. Tsaroukian was angered by a report that his French business partner in a brewing venture had ordered him not to present himself as chairman. (RFE/RL)

The Yerevan office of the Russian-language newspaper *Novoe Vremya* was badly damaged in a 31 December fire. Editor **Ruben Satyan** said he had received telephone threats prior to the arson attack. ITAR-TASS linked the incident to the reprinting in *Novoe Vremya* of an article from a Moscow publication concerning the 27 October murder of Premier Vazgen Sargsian. (RFE/RL)

On 27 January **Nikol Pashinian** was given a one-year suspended sentence by the Yerevan High Court for insulting law enforcement officials, failing to publish a retraction and slandering two persons. Pashinian and the *Haykakan Zhamanak* newspaper, formerly called *Oragir*, lost a series of libel suits in

1999 to individuals close to the authorities (*Index* 2/1999, 4/1999, 6/1999). (RFE/RL)

AUSTRALIA

It was reported on 8 December that the Australian Broadcasting Corporation and the *Age* newspaper are being investigated by the intelligence services after publicising a series of stories on East Timor based on intelligence leaks. The investigation could lead to criminal charges. One allegation is that the government was far better informed than it admitted of the role of the Indonesian military in fomenting militia violence before the independence ballot on 30 August. This conflicts with government testimony in a Senate inquiry. (Inter Press Service)

Electronic Frontiers Australia (EFA), has moved its website to the US after the government gave its approval to a Code of Practice for Internet service providers, it was reported on 21 December. Internet users are now required to install filters on their computers, which are designed to block many websites. The lists of blocked sites are kept secret from Internet surfers and site owners. (EFA)

AZERBAIJAN

Christian missionaries should be banned from proselytising according to Muzaffar Jebrailzade, a member of the Supreme Council of the Islamic Party of Azerbaijan, who called on President Heidar Aliyev to decree such a ban. Jebrailzade told an 18 January meeting that 10,000 Azeris had already been

converted to Christianity by representatives of 'over 1,000 missionary organisations', many 'disguised as humanitarian groups'. (RFE/RL, Turan)

At the end of January, the authorities launched a new attempt to seize the assets of the independent station Radio-TV Sara, including its broadcast antenna and equipment worth more than US$500,000. The attempted seizure comes after the station's refusal to pay a US$62,000 fine (*Index* 6/1999, 1/2000). (A19)

BANGLADESH

On 30 November the offices of *Weekly Evidence*, an English-language publication, were ransacked by unknown attackers for the third time in a year. Police later searched the home of the managing editor, who went into hiding on the same day. According to **Manzoor Quader**, the editor and a leader of the opposition Bangladesh Nationalist Party, the paper has been targeted by members of the government. *Weekly Evidence* was suspended from publishing on 28 November because the editor's address was written incorrectly in the newspaper. (RSF)

On 8 December police stepped in to protect **Monir Haider** of *Dainik Janakantha*, **Muhaamad Alam** of *Dainik Ajker Kagoj*, **Saleh Uddin** of *Manav Zamin* and **Amlan Dewan** of *Bhorer Kagoj* from attack by militants of the ruling Awami League during municipal elections in Kishoreganj. The journalists had recently criticised violations of the election rules. The following day **Bahauddin**, a bookseller and correspondent for *Ajker* Kagoj, was also threatened by members of the Awami League. He had denounced irregularities in the local elections. (RSF/WAN)

Over a dozen journalists were seriously injured by activists of the opposition Islamic Oikya Jote at an anti-government demonstration in Chittagong on 12 December. The attack followed a speech denouncing the press by Mufti Izharul Islam, leader of the movement. Among the journalists injured were **Rafiquk Bahar** of *Dainik Prothom Alo*, **Helal Uddin** of *Dainik Azadi Kagoj*, **Nasirul Haq** of the daily *Arthaniti*, **Mainuddin Dulal** of *Azadi*, **Mohammed Ali** of *Purbokone*, **Kazi Abu Mansur** of the daily *Janakantha* and photojournalists **Mustafizur Rahman** of *Ittefaq* daily and **Rashed Ahmed** of *Prothom Alo*. (Media Watch, RSF, WAN)

Also on 12 December **Sanaullah Labloo** of *Dainik Prothom Alo* was taken to hospital with head injuries after he was assaulted by Awami League activists at his office. (RSF)

On 24 December **Timir Lal Dutta** of *Dainik Khabar* daily, **Rafiqul Sabuj** of Bangladesh News Service, **Mamum-ur Rashid** of *Manav Zamin* and **Siddique Islam** of *Banglar Bani* were taken to hospital with gunshot wounds after attending a meeting of a newly created opposition party in Dhaka. Ruling party Awami League activists were responsible for the attack. (RSF)

Anu Muhammod, editor of online magazine meghbarta.net,

was arrested on 26 December. He was attending a conference in Chittagong. (RSF)

On 1 January **Anwar Hossain** of *Banglabazar Patrika* daily and **Anwar-al-din** of *Ittefaq* daily received death threats from members of the Chattra League – the student wing of the Awami party. The two journalists were accused of damaging the reputation of Chattra League leader Sazzad Hossain. (Media Watch)

Azadi daily was damaged by two bomb blasts on 4 January. After the first bomb blast the unknown attackers threw a second, damaging the managing editor's car. (Media Watch)

Zakir Hossain Sumon-Srinagar of *Ajker Kagoj* daily and **Shafi-uddin Ahmed** were attacked on 5 January by members of Chattra Dal – the student wing of opposition Bangladesh Nationalist Party. Ahmed, a senior journalist and former president of the Bangladesh Journalists Association, had stepped in to protect his colleague who was accused of publishing information critical of Chattra Dal. (Media Watch)

On 15 January **Mir Illais Hossain**, publisher and editor of *Dainik Bir Darpan*, was shot and killed by three masked attackers in the city of Jhenaidah. Hossain, who was also the leader of the leftist Sramajibi Mukti Andolan party, had received death threats a few weeks earlier from Maoist armed movements who he had criticised in print. (RSF)

Publisher **Mohammad Imtiaz**

Amin was arrested on 5 February after a booklet he published sparked intra-Muslim violence in Khulna the day before. *Allah ki Niakar? Sarbatra Birajoman? (Is God Shapeless? Does he exist everywhere?)* by **Moulana Abdur Rauf** was published by the minority Ahle Hadis sect and contains references likely to offend mainstream Sunni Muslims. (Agence France Press)

BELARUS

It was reported on 10 January that Leanid Levin, a leader of the Jewish community in Belarus, is to sue the Minsk publishing house for publishing the book *The War According to the Laws of Meanness*, a compendium of anti-Semitic articles from the Russian and Belarusian press which Levin believes foment ethnic hatred. (RFE/RL)

BENIN

Vincent Foly, editor of the daily *Le Point*, was detained and imprisoned in the civil jail of Cotonou on 26 January. In September 1999, while working for the daily *Le Matin*, Foly was sentenced to 12 months in prison after the publication of an article revealing misappropriation of funds. (RSF)

BRAZIL

Five photo-journalists were severely beaten by military police officers while covering the end-of-year activities at Copacabana Fort, attended by President Fernando Henrique Cardoso. **Fernando Bizerra** of *Jornal do Brasil*, **Edivaldo Ferreira** and **José Paulo Lacerda** of Agencia Estado, **Sheila Chagas**, a freelancer with Editora Abril, and **Rosa Costa** of Agencia Estado, were attacked while photographing a discussion with one of the local base commanders. Bizerra was also threatened with death. (IFJ)

Some 2,000 community radio stations in Sao Paulo state were ordered by a federal judge to close by 6 February for allegedly interfering with the radio signals of overflying aircraft. A senior official of the Regional Flight Protection Service denied that the broadcasts interfered with flights. (World Association of Community Radio Broadcasters)

BULGARIA

On 17 January President Petar Stoyanov vetoed a law, passed by parliament a week earlier, that would have imposed heavy fines upon journalists found guilty for libel or slander. (RFE/RL)

BURMA

It was reported on 21 January that Myanmar Post and Telecoms has applied a new restriction to the use of Internet and e-mail for communicating political commentaries and information 'detrimental to the government'. The information comes after two private Internet service providers were closed and three people were arrested for consulting opposition websites in foreign countries. (RSF)

CHECHNYA

The identification of a cameraman for the Grozny-based Nokh Cho TV station, who died in a Russian rocket attack on 2 December, was incorrect (*Index*

1/2000). His name was not Shamil Yegayev but **Shamil Gigayev.** (CPJ)

Three Russian and six foreign journalists were apprehended on 29 December near the village of Pervomaiskoye, north-west on Grozny, and held for several hours after accusations that they were travelling to a combat area without official accreditation. **Marcus Warren** of the British *Daily Telegraph,* **Daniel Williams** of the *Washington Post,* **David Filipov** of the daily *Boston Globe,* **Rodrigo Fernandez** with the Spanish daily *El País,* **Ricardo Ortega** of the Spanish television channel *Antena 3* and his cameraman **Teimuraz Gabashvili** were taken to the military base in Mozdok and, when released, were ordered to leave Chechnya. (RFE/RL)

CENTRAL AFRICAN REPUBLIC

President Ange-Félix Patasse said on 28 December that, from 1 January, 'measures will be taken against the press, which has a tendency to incite rebellion, tribal war and hatred'. He added that 'the page has definitively been turned and recess is over'. (RSF)

CHINA

Two hundred of China's 2,000 provincial newspapers are due to be closed down in the first half of this year. Those targeted – tabloids specialising in judiciary, police, security and social matters – will be merged into one tabloid per province, managed directly by provincial agencies. Twenty seven newspapers have so far been 'punished' for violating

press regulations, *Xinhua* reported on 12 January. Some were closed down but the nature of other punishments was not stipulated. Violations included the publishing of stories with 'political errors', sensationalism and fabricating stories. **Jiang Yiping**, editor of *Southern Weekend,* was removed from her post on or around 10 January. On 26 January the respected Beijing journal *Hundred Year Tide* was 'served warning' by ideology and propaganda officials. A vociferous advocate of quickening reform, the journal is expecting to have staff installed by the government following the retirement of the director, **Zheng Hui**, in January. (Associated Press. RSF, Reuters. *South China Morning Post*)

The China Democracy Party (CDP), most of whose founders were sentenced to long prison terms on charges of subversion last year (*Index* 5/1999, 6/1999), released a statement on 24 December calling for sweeping democratic reforms in China. The statement's author, **He Depu** (*Index* 5/1999), is still at liberty. Nineteen-year-old **Wang Yingzheng** (*Index* 3/1999) was sentenced to three years in prison in late December on charges of subversion for photocopying a self-penned article about official corruption. Wang was a protégé of **Qin Yongmin** (*Index* 2/1999), jailed for 12 years in December for his part in organising a Jiangsu branch of the CDP. **Tong Shidong**, an assistant professor of physics at Hunan University, and **Liao Shihua**, a factory worker from Hunan, were sentenced to prison for ten and six years respectively, also on charges of subversion. **Dai Xuezhong**, a CDP activist from Shanghai, was sentenced to prison for three years on charges of assault in what fellow political activists claim to be a 'cynical frame-up'. (Agence-France Presse. Associated Press. Reuters, Information Centre of Human Rights and Democratic Movements in China)

The arrest of *Falun Gong* practitioners continued unabated throughout mainland China. Four leaders were tried and sentenced in Beijing on 26 December for 'using a cult to undermine laws, causing deaths and illegally obtaining and disseminating state secrets'. They are **Yao Jie**, sentenced to seven years, **Ji Liewu**, 12 years, **Wang Zhiwen**, 16 years and **Li Chang**, sentenced to 18 years. Li was accused of organising the original demonstration by 10,000 people in Beijing in April 1999 (*Index* 5/1999). **Zhang Chunqing**, a 22-year-old student, was re-arrested in Dalian, Liaoning, in late December and sent to labour camp for three years for posting an image of her bloodied ankles on a website after she had been forced to walk in 10kg shackles. **Li Fujun**, an assistant professor of medicine in Henan (*Index* 6/1999), was sentenced to four years in prison on 3 January for 'using a cult to undermine laws,' organising a protest on Tiananmen Square and posting an article on a foreign website. **Xu Xinmu**, a public official and *Falun Gong* practitioner, was sentenced to four years in prison on the same day for leaking the text of a speech by President Jiang Zemin in June announcing the impending crackdown against *Falun Gong*. State radio announced on 6 January that **Xu**

Xianglan was sentenced to eight years for organising and attending meetings in Wuhan, while her husband, **Wang Hansheng**, was sentenced to six years for assisting her. Also on 6 January, **General Yu Changxin**, a prominent and highly respected 74-year-old retired air-force officer, was sentenced to 17 years' imprisonment for his part in organising the Beijing demonstration. **Gao Xianmin**, one of ten members arrested on 31 December, was pronounced dead on arrival at hospital in Guangzhou on 17 January. He had gone on hunger strike to protest beatings in custody, but was forced to drink salt water, causing his internal organs to fail. **Liu Zhilan**, detained on 10 January, was forced to clean offices in the police station where she was held in Beijing. She died on 14 January after breathing gases in a furnace room. It was reported on 21 January that as many as 50 practitioners are continuing more than seven weeks' 're-education' in a psychiatric hospital outside Beijing. Sixteen people – one from Macao, three from Hong Kong and 12 from China – were arrested on 24 Jan while unfurling a 20-foot portrait of **Li Hongzhi**, founder of the movement, to cover the portrait of Chairman Mao overlooking Tiananmen Square. On 28 January a total of 32 people were sentenced to prison on charges brought under the 'anti-cult' legislation. Two sisters, **Li Xiaobing and Li Xiaomei**, were sentenced to six and seven years respectively. They owned a video shop in Beijing which, according to the prosecution, was a front for selling 1.8 million books on *Falun Gong* and were

thought to be closely associated with the Beijing leadership. The other 30 were sentenced to terms of between four months and two years. Between 100 and 300 protesters attempted to stage a protest in Tiananmen Square soon after midnight on 5 February – the beginning of the Lunar New Year. Police responded immediately, running into the group of people and kicking and dragging them away to waiting vans. (Agence-France Presse. Associated Press, BBC, Reuters, *VIP Reference.*)

In a deliberate snub to the Vatican on 6 January, Beijing arrested five Chinese bishops on the same day that the Pope ordained 12 in Rome. The Connecticut-based Cardinal Joseph Kung Foundation reported on 23 January that five members of China's underground Catholic church are being held in detention for 'illegal religious activities'. Bishop **Han Dingxiang** from Hebei, who has spent 20 of his 65 years in prison, was arrested on or around 1 December. **Wang Chenqun**, a layman from Hebei who has spent ten of the last 20 years in prison or labour camps, was arrested 'shortly before Christmas'. Two priests, **Guo Yibao** and **Wang Zhenhe**, are reported to be in a Hebei detention centre having been arrested on their way to deliver mass over Easter 1999. The whereabouts of the priest **Xie Guolin**, also detained in 1999, are unknown. (Associated Press, Cardinal Joseph Kung Foundation)

On 12 January the government began broadcasting programmes in Mandarin and interference over the same short-wave frequency used by the Norwegian-based Voice of Tibet (VOT), jamming their signal. VOT immediately changed their frequency, but on 23 January it was jammed again. (Agence-France Presse, RSF)

Qazhyqumar Shabdanuly, a dissident Kazakh writer from Xinjiang, was reportedly released from prison in mid-January. Shabdanuly, 76, has spent some 50 years in Chinese prisons. No details had been made available on his case since he was last sentenced in 1988. (RFE/RL, AI)

Song Yongyi, a US resident and librarian-scholar at Dickinson College, Pennsylvania, was released from detention nearly six months after his arrest on 7 August. He was charged on 24 Dec with 'endangering national security' and 'revealing state secrets' – charges apparently relating to a body of research he had amassed, and planned to take home, on his specialised field, the Cultural Revolution. His wife, **Helen Yao**, who was also arrested but released earlier, said the material had been collected from public sources, such as archived newspapers, pamphlets and street markets. One western source suggested Yongi was arrested because his research seemed to indicate that Zhou Enlai, an almost saintly figure and adoptive father to current Prime Minister Li Peng, played a more ruthless role in the Cultural Revolution than is generally ascribed. (Associated Press. BBC. Reuters. *VIP Reference*)

Two more cults have been criminalised. On 16 January it

was reported that the China Gospel Fellowship, an underground Christian family church in Henan, had been branded 'an evil cult' by the State Council. Six of the church's leaders have been sent to labour camps, including **Zhang Rongliang** and **Shen Yiping**. The government has also conducted a low-key campaign since November 1999 against a group called *Zhong Gong*, which is similar in practice to *Falun Gong*. The first known arrest is that of **Chen Jinlong**, a regional leader from Zhejiang, sentenced to two years in prison on 19 January for 'illegally practising medicine'. *Zhong Gong* claims ten million members in 20 provinces. Its leader, **Zhang Hongbao**, is in hiding. (Associated Press, BBC, *Daily Telegraph*, *Hong Kong Standard*)

On 26 January the *People's Daily* published a set of new regulations governing use of the Internet. Issued by the little-known State Secrecy Bureau, the regulations effectively impose the same strict measures against Internet service providers as those levelled at the print media, whereby vaguely defined 'state secrets' cannot be up- or down-loaded or even discussed over the Internet. It is reported that more regulations putting a similar onus on to Internet content providers (ICPs) are imminent, obliging ICPs to reproduce only news which has been previously vetted. In a related move, regulations quietly published in October require all companies, organisations and individuals – both foreign and Chinese – which use encryption software to register not only which brand of software is used, but also the name, address and

identification details of the persons using it. (Associated Press, *ChinaOnline.com*, Reuters)

COLOMBIA

Pablo Emilio Medina Motta, a cameraman with regional station TV Garzón, was killed by multiple shots to the head and back when more than 100 guerrillas from the Revolutionary Armed Forces of Colombia stormed the town of Gigante, Huila, on 4 December. Medina reportedly jumped on a motorcycle driven by a police commander to get a better vantage point of the fire-fight. It is assumed that the guerrillas mistook him for a member of the security forces. (CPJ)

Daily El Tiempo correspondent **Carlos Augusto Pulgarín Guevara** fled to Peru on 7 December after repeated death threats from paramilitaries. The threats started in June after Pulgarín denounced the slaughter of Embera Katío Indians in Córdoba and filed reports on the conflict there that contradicted death-toll figures announced by paramilitary organisation Autodefensas Unidas de Colombia (AUC). This earned him the derogatory label of 'the guerrilla's press relations man'. After fleeing Córdoba, Pulgarín was kidnapped and verbally abused at gunpoint by a group of men. The 29-year-old journalist has continued to receive death threats in Lima. (IPYS)

Journalist **Margarita Gómez Albarello** has made a public appeal for help after having to flee the country because of threats from paramilitary groups. In a letter received on 4 January,

Gómez said that she was first threatened on 20 October while working for the daily *El Nuevo Día* in Ibagué, covering the armed conflict between guerrillas, paramilitaries and the army. A few days later she fled to Bogotá. The threats continued, however, and she left the country for the US on 5 December. (National Centre for Social Communication)

Journalist **Edgardo Montenegro**, from the Cali-based daily *El Caleño*, survived an attempt on his life on 21 January by two unidentified armed assailants on motorcycles. Montenegro was hit by a bullet after being shot at four times in front of his house. (CPJ)

Concern is mounting for **Guillermo Cortés**, head of television news programme *Hora Cero*, who was kidnapped on 22 January by six armed men at his weekend home. Nothing has been heard from the 78-year-old journalist since, and nobody has claimed responsibility for the kidnap. (CPJ)

CONGO BRAZZAVILLE

Radio France International and RSF correspondent **Alain Shungu Ngongo** was threatened by Finance Minister Marthias Dzon at the conclusion of a press conference held in Brazzaville. The minister declared Ngongo as his 'enemy'. Since early January Ngongo has investigated the possible embezzlement of public funds within the Directorate General of Taxation. (RSF)

COTE D'IVOIRE

On 27 December **Jean-Baptiste Akrou** and **Gaoussou Kamissoko**, journalists with the government daily *Fraternité Matin*, were arrested in their offices in Abidjan. No explanation was given. The head of the daily's administration was also detained. Akrou and Kamissoko were freed a few hours after being detained. The authorities reported that the journalists were arrested by 'an uncontrolled group' that was acting on its own initiative. (RSF)

CUBA

Cuban state security officers arrested four journalists and placed another six under house arrest on 16-17 December in an apparent attempt to prevent coverage of an anti-government demonstration in Havana. Journalists **Juan González Febles**, **Adela Soto Alvarez**, **María del Carmen Carro** and **Santiago Martínez Trujillo** were taken into custody the day before the peaceful march was scheduled to take place on 17 December. On the morning before the planned demonstration, another six journalists – **Meri Miranda**, **Osvaldo de Céspedes**, **María de los Angeles Gómez**, **Amarylis Cortina**, **Ricardo González** and **Alida Viso** – were put under house arrest. All ten have since been released. (CPJ)

CZECH REPUBLIC

On 12 December the State Attorney's Office in Prague launched a lawsuit against **Zdenek Zukal**, owner and director of the private television studio *ZZIP* in Olomouc, for making 'false accusations' against police officers. Police have harassed Zukal since his first series of investigative reports broadcast on TV Nova in 1997, which linked law enforcement officials with organised crime. (CPJ)

Jakub Puchalsky, director general of state-owned Czech Television, has resigned after less than two years in charge, it was reported on 17 December. Puchalsky said he had been subject to constant attempts at political interference, particularly from deputies of the powerful opposition Civic Democratic party. (*Financial Times*)

DEMOCRATIC REPUBLIC OF CONGO

Gaspard Biala Linoga and **Jacques Bololo**, heads respectively of subscriptions and distribution for the occasional satirical magazine *Pot-Pourri*, were arrested in Kinshasa's Victoria Square on 8 December. The arrests were connected to Edition 52 of *Pot-Pourri* which contained an article, 'AIDS in the National Palace' that denounced President Laurent Kabila's 'embezzlement system'. The two men were taken to unknown destinations and copies of Edition 52 were confiscated along with the day's earnings. Bololo was released later the same evening, but Linoga remains in solitary confinement. (Journaliste en Danger)

According to reports on 7 January the managing director of the thrice-weekly *La Libre Afrique*, **Freddy Loseke**

Simon Davies on

PRIVACY

Ursula Owen on

HATE SPEECH

Patricia Williams on

RACE

Gabriel Garcia Marquez on

JOURNALISM

Edward Lucie-Smith on

THE INTERNET

...all in INDEX

SUBSCRIBE & SAVE

SUBSCRIBE & SAVE

CONGO BRAZZAVILLE – ETHIOPIA

Lisumbu La Yayenga, was arrested by soldiers and held in solitary confinement at Kokolo barracks. Sources connected the arrests with two articles in the 28 and 31 December editions. The first stated that 'a general in Kantaga wants to assassinate [President] Kabila'; the second was entitled 'A mutiny is being organised to prompt Kabila's flight'. (Journaliste en Danger)

On 25 January **Jérome Debo** a member of the Journaliste en Danger (JED) media monitoring group, narrowly escaped abduction at a bus stop in Bandalungwa district of Kinshasa. The JED's secretariat have also received threatening telephone calls. The threats came 12 days after the kidnapping of lawyer and human rights activist **Kayeme Kasuku** from the head office of the External Department of the National Information Agency. (JED)

On 24 January journalist **Norbert Tambwe** of the daily *Tempête des Tropiques* was summoned for questioning to the Special Services Branch in Kinshasa. Tambwe said the case involved an article in the 21 January edition entitled 'Two presidential escort motorcyclists killed after speeding'. Tambwe had written that the two escorts caused several major accidents as a result of the speeding that led to their deaths on 18 January. (JED)

Sports journalist **Gérard Desiré Angenwa Agbeme**, managing editor of the *Voix de la Verité*, appeared in court without a lawyer on 1 February to fight a suit for 'harmful accusations' filed by Olivie Bielaire, Tambwe

Lombe and Tshamala Kazadi Tshamy, technical personnel of the football team Daring Club Motema Pembe. The journalist had called them a 'band of adventurers and fetishist sports swindlers'. (JED)

EAST TIMOR

On 27 January an Australian coroner concluded that freelance Dutch journalist **Sander Thoenes** (*Index* 6/1999) was indeed killed by Indonesian troops last year. An inquest into the death had been delayed by a lack of witnesses from the Indonesian military. Sander Thoenes, who worked for the *Christian Science Monitor* and *Financial Times*, was killed on 21 September, the day after the first foreign peacekeeping force arrived to restore order. (Associated Press, PINA)

EGYPT

Magdy Hussein, **Saleh Bedewi** and **Essam Eddine Hanafi** (*Index* 3/1998, 4/1998, 5/1998, 6/1998, 4/1999, 5/1999), jailed for libel in August, were released on 5 December. The three journalists were sentenced to two years' imprisonment and fined E£20,000 (US$5,900) and damages of E£501 (US$150) for libelling Agriculture Minister and Deputy Prime Minister Youssef Wali in August last year. The court ruled that the journalists had not been given a free trial and ordered a retrial. (CPJ)

On 19 January the Egyptian Organisation for Human Rights (EOHR) learned for the first time of the imminent closure of its newsletter *Hououkul-insan*

when a banning decree was served by the Misr Al-Kadim police station. The order, issued in September 1999 by the Governor of Cairo, banned a further 13 publications. (Egyptian Organisation for Human Rights)

ETHIOPIA

Bizunesh Debebe remains in prison notwithstanding the Federal High Court order of 12 December 1999 for her release after she paid her bail (*Index* 1/2000). (IFJ)

Abera Wogi, editor-in-chief of the private weekly *Maebe*, was sentenced on 23 December to a year's imprisonment. Having been detained since 12 May, he is now due for release in May 2000. Abera was charged with defamation and 'fabrication and dissemination of false information' in connection with a profile of a general exiled in Sudan, who accused Prime Minister Meles Zenawi of killing 80 people with cyanide when he was fighting against the government of former President Haile Mengistu. (RSF)

On 25 January **Tesahalene Mengesha** (*Index* 5/1999) deputy editor of the private weekly *Mebruk*, was sentenced to one year in prison for 'defamation of news' and violation of the press law. Four years ago Tesahalene revealed the identities of high-level military appointments two months before the government made them public. His conviction came as a total surprise since the article was later made public by the state media. (RSF)

INDEX ON CENSORSHIP 2 2000   99

●●●●●●●●●●●●●●●●●●●●●●●●●●●●●●●●●●●

VIRGILIO DA SILVA GUTERRES
Shadows

Last year was a turning point for the people of Timor Lorosae. We ought to be happy because what we have always dreamt of, and fought so hard for with our lives, is already here. But problems persist.

They range from political reconciliation to rebuilding from scratch the country's economic, political and social infrastructure. However, if we are not vigilant we might enter an era of neo-colonisation – this time by outside forces beyond our control.

Interfet, UNTAET, UNHCR, OCHA (Office for the Coordination of Humanitarian Affairs), etc have been in Timor Lorosae for four months but workable systems are yet to be implemented. In many parts, people are dying of malnourishment because aid from the UN did not reach them.

The Council for the National East Timorese Resistance (CNRT) also keeps people in the dark. We eagerly await to hear CNRT's plans for kick-starting the economy and political reconciliation, but to no avail. In the cases of language and currency, it's clearly a matter of a tiny minority trying to impose their will on a majority. While Tetun is the lingua franca, these political elites insist on Portuguese and the adoption of the escudo.

Our political leaders have to respect the rights of the people to be in the know as to what decisions are made in their name. They have the right to be informed and the right to question.

For a people which has suffered over decades of extreme hardship under the Indonesians, we long for a good life free from misery and brutality. For that good life, we need to search within ourselves and within our country. Don't depend on everything that comes from Australia, Portugal or the US. And don't let the World Bank or Branco Naçional Ultramarino Portugal dictate terms on how our economy should be kick-started.

But the harsh reality remains: we, at last, won in the referendum, but still remain unable to govern ourselves and our country. Why? The simple reason: We are NOT given the opportunity to be leaders in our own country! ❏

Virgilio da Silva Guterres *is editor of East Timor's first Tetun-language paper* Lalenok, *which hit the streets on 18 January. This is an edited extract from his first editorial,* Leno An' (Shadows).

●●●●●●●●●●●●●●●●●●●●●●●●●●●●●●●●

Journalist **Makonnen Worku** has committed suicide, it was reported on 28 January. A member of the Ethiopian Free Press Journalists Association and former chief editor of the weekly *Maebe*, Makonnen was detained for a long period in Addis Ababa prison for alleged violations of the Press Law, but had recently been released on bail. Lately new charges were instituted against him and police were reportedly searching for him. (IFJ)

FIJI

Russell Hunter, the Scottish editor-in-chief of the *Fiji Times*, was given 28 days to leave the country on 28 December after his application for a renewal of his work permit was refused (*Index* 1/2000). Home Affairs Minister Joji Uluinakauvadra said there were locals who could fill the position. But on 12 January the *Times* was allowed to apply for a judicial review after its lawyer claimed the decision was 'actuated by unreasonable, extraneous or improper considerations'. (PINA)

On 20 December senior cabinet minister Ganesh Chand accused 'certain journalists' of carrying out a campaign to destabilise the government. A story had appeared that day in the *Fiji Times* in which acting Prime Minister Tupeni Baba called on Prime Minister Mahendra Chaudry to clear the air over recent controversies concerning Chaudry himself and the government. Chand also claimed that an interview and editorial in *Sunday Times* had suggested that Baba was starting to look like an 'alternative prime minister'. (PINA)

Rajendra Chaudry, son of Prime Minister Mahendra Chaudry, is planning legal action against **Margaret Wise** (*Index* 1/2000), a reporter on the *Fiji Times*, for alleged unethical conduct, it was reported on 21 January. She had accused Chaudry jr of 'jacking-up a government-paid trip to Germany' in order that he could attend a Socialist party meeting at the government's expense after it had granted him leave for the trip, but refused to pay for it. (*Pacific Media Watch*, PINA)

FRANCE

On 14 December **Hubert Levet**, a contributor to the economics daily *AGEFI*, was detained following a complaint by the directors of Aérospatiale-Matra for 'divulging confidential financial information'. The journalist was held for questioning, then examined by a preliminary judge of the High Court of Paris before being released. On the same day, the financial squad searched the offices of *AGEFI*. This occurred following the 21 September publication of an official document presenting Aérospatiale-Matra's semi-annual accounts. (RSF)

A report by an anti-sect government committee described the Church of Scientology as 'a dangerous organisation that threatens public order and human dignity' on 7 February. It also called for the organisation to be dissolved. (*Guardian*)

GABON

On 22 December **Germain Lendoye**, a journalist with the private weekly *Cigale Enchantée*, was arrested for publishing an article last March entitled 'The irremovable Duke of Mounana' in which he accused Minister for Public Works Zacharie Myboto of having 'run off with the property of the district' of Mounana. Lendoye and the newspaper's publishing head, **Dorothee Ngouoni**, were sentenced last July to two months in prison and ordered to pay a fine. Fearing reprisals, Ngouoni had since fled. (RSF)

GHANA

Stephen Owusu, editor of *Free Press*, was sentenced to one day in prison on 31 January for publishing a story about an active court case in which two rival shareholders of Ashanti Goldfields Company (AGC) are seeking to unseat the board of directors. On 26 January, *Free Press* announced that two more shareholders were joining the case and that this reinforced the shareholders' dissatisfaction with the board and management of the company. The story revealed that, while the company's fortunes declined, board members and top management were securing lucrative AGC contracts. Owusu was reprimanded for carrying out an investigation into an active court case. (Free Expression Ghana)

Kabral Blay Amihere, president of the West African Journalists Association (WAJA) and editor of the *Independent*, was arrested and held overnight on 13 January by military personnel following an article to which the military objected. Amihere was forced to publish a rejoinder in the paper pre-prepared by the army. (WAJA)

GREECE

Evangelical radio station Channel 2000 was forcibly shut down on 20 December and **Lakis Regas**, a retired pastor who was working there as a technician, was arrested. Police wanted to confiscate the transmitters, but they took the main satellite instead. But no private radio station is able to acquire a licence and specialists found the allegations of disruption to be untrue. Days before the raid the Greek Orthodox Church had accused the station of 'dangerous proselytism'. (*Greek Helsinki Monitor*)

GUATEMALA

Larry Lee, Guatemala City correspondent for business agency Bridge News, was found dead on 28 December in his apartment with several knife wounds in his throat and abdomen. Lee had been in Guatemala for a year and is believed to have been planning to relocate to Mexico. (RSF)

GUINEA

Saliou Samb, editor-in-chief of *L'Indépendent Plus*, was arrested on 15 December and expelled to Ghana nearly two weeks later. No explanation for the arrest and expulsion was given. However, the measures are the latest in a series of 'legal' actions against the press group since the publication in early December of an investigation on corruption implicating the government. On 4 December **Aboubacar Sylla**, owner of *L'Indépendent* and *L'Indépendent Plus*, was arrested and released two days later. On 7 December, the police closed the offices of the publications and two days later seized all copies of *L'Indépendent*. (RSF)

HUNGARY

The editor of the independent weekly *Elet es Irodalom* believes that an attack on the offices on 27 December came in reprisal for a recent court victory in a libel suit filed against it by Prime Minister Viktor Orban and the governing Party Fidesz. The suit concerned the paper's publication on 20 August of an article alleging that the party had financially benefited from the privatisation of a mining company and the sale of public buildings in the early 1990s. **Eva Vajda,** who authorised the articles, has already been under police investigation for publishing articles in mid-1999 detailing how the state-controlled Postabank provided preferential loans and accounts to a VIP list. (CPJ, RFE/RL)

INDIA

Author **Arundhati Roy** was among 400 protesters arrested on 11 January for 'defying prohibitory orders' when they tried to block the controversial Narmada Dam project in Madhya Pradesh state. Roy's action is a direct challenge to recent strictures placed upon her and other activists by the Supreme Court (*Index* 6/1999). (*Guardian*)

The film *Water* again ran into trouble on 6 February after Arun Pathak, a Shiv Sainik cadre, tried to commit suicide in protest against the film being shot in the holy city of Varanasi. Violence subsequently broke out and city authorities asked director **Deepa** **Mehta** and her crew to leave immediately. On 19 January the Uttar Pradesh government considered stopping Mehta from filming after two ministers stated that the script of *Water* is 'too hot to handle'. (*Asian Age*)

IRAN

It was reported on 27 December that reformist cleric and ally of President Khatami, **Abdullah Nouri**, imprisoned for dissent in November (*Index* 1/2000), may be eligible to stand in the 18 February parliamentary elections according to Interior Minister Abdul-Vahed Mussavi-Lari. (*International Herald Tribune*)

On 4 January **Said Hajarian**, editor of the reformist daily *Sobh Emrooz*, was prosecuted by Tehran's Press Court after the secret service and the army lodged a number of complaints, including that he had 'disclosed confidential information'. No further specifics were given. (RSF, WAN)

Said Haajarian appeared before the Press Court again on 16 January, along with editors **Yadollah Eslami** and **Ghafour Garchasebi** of the reformist dailies *Fath* and *Asr-azadegan*, for having reprinted an interview with the banned cleric **Ayatollah Ali Hossein Montazeri**, which originally appeared in the British *Guardian* on 13 January. In the interview, Montazeri 'called for the powers of the country's supreme leader to be curbed and greater respect for people's right to determine their own destiny'. He also described the conservative-controlled Council of Guardians' disqualification of 401 candidates for the 18

● ●

HOSSEIN BAGHER ZADEH
Death to abolitionists

On 24 August 1999 I published an article in the mass circulation daily in Tehran, *Nesaht,* entitled 'Is State Violence Permissible?', in which I argued against capital punishment in Iran. The article led to a huge outcry by certain politico-religious groups, implying that I had taken a position against the Islamic laws of vengeance (I had made no reference to these or any other religious laws in the article). Iran's leader Ayatollah Ali Khamenei made a statement on 1 September denouncing those 'who oppose the religious law of vengeance' as 'apostates' and declaring them liable to the death sentence. Three days later, the authorities shut down *Neshat,* and the head of the judiciary, Ayatollah Shahroodi, referred to me as an 'infidel and corrupt' individual and declared my article to be offensive to Islam.

These official declarations prompted several state-sponsored newspapers to call me an apostate and demand my execution. They also fabricated some slanderous accusations against me related to the events in the 1970s. Finally, on 11 September, the weekly *Jebheh,* mouthpiece of Ansar-e Hezbollah (a group associated with Ayatollah Khamenei) called for a formal fatwa and declared a bounty of 100m rials (approx. US$33,000) for anybody who carries out the death sentence. There has been no official condemnation of this public incitement to murder, or any indication of prosecuting its perpetrators.

These attacks and fabricated stories were quoted in almost all the dailies. When I tried to refute the allegations, none would print my denials (with the exception of an English-language daily). In effect, I have become a 'forbidden writer' who cannot refute the false accusations, which have been repeated again and again since then.

The government has failed to condemn this action or even to disassociate itself from it. ❏

Hossein Bagher Zadeh is the London-based chair of the steering committee of the Iranian Human Rights Working Group (www.ihrwg.org). Neshat *publisher Latif Safari and its chief editor Mashallah Shams-ol-Vaezin were sentenced to suspended prison terms and banned from journalism for five years*

● ●

February parliamentary elections as unconstitutional. The majority were barred on the grounds that they are 'allegedly not committed to Islam and the political system'. (*Middle East International*, RSF)

On 3 February hundreds of clerics and seminary students protested in Qom over a newspaper cartoon mocking the leading ideologue of the right, Ayatollah Mohammad Taqi Mesbah-Yazdi. (*Observer*)

IRAQ

On 9 December two unidentified gunmen shot **Hawjin Mala Amin** in front of his home in Suleymania, southern Kurdistan. Hawjin, a Kurdish intellectual and researcher at the University of Suleymania, was shot four times and remains in a local hospital. (Kurdistan Observer, Kurdish Media)

On 1 January the Patriotic Union of Kurdistan (PUK) launched a television satellite channel, KurdSat, to broadcast to the southern Kurdish regions. Last year, the Kurdistan Democratic Party (KDP) also launched a satellite service, KTV, allegedly supported by Turkey in a bid to rival Medya-TV (formerly Med-TV (*Index* 2/1997, 5/1997, 6/1998, 1/1999). (Kurdistan Observer)

Studying or speaking in Kurdish or Turkomen has been banned in all schools in Kirkuk, by order of the Office of the Presidency. On 19 January a decree was issued by the Directorate of Education prompting protests from both ethnic communities. Kurdish newspaper *Rizgari* claimed the decision was part of an enforced

'displacement order against Kurds and others'. (RFE/RL Iraq Report)

The state-owned *Al-Iraq* daily reported on 28 January that there would be nationwide parliamentary elections on 27 March, the first since 1996. Candidates are forbidden from holding rallies, publishing manifestos or speaking on television. (Associated Press)

ISRAEL

Ofer Nimrodi (*Index* 1/2000), publisher of Ma-ariv news agency, was charged by Tel Aviv District Court on 26 December with conspiracy to murder a private investigator who had testified against him in a wire-tapping case. (*New York Times*)

Palestinian photographer **Atta Wiesat** was attacked by plain-clothes intelligence agents on 3 January. Wiesat, who worked for the Israeli press agency Zoom 77, was struck and his camera broken while taking pictures of the arrest of a Palestinian close to Damascus Gate, Jerusalem. He was taken to al-Hadassa Hospital where he received emergency care. (RSF)

On 8 January the Council of Sages were reported to have been issued a ruling banning the Internet from Jewish households in an attempt to prevent the spread of 'sin and abomination' into ultra-orthodox homes. (*DailyTelegraph*)

JAPAN

The Chinese government has repeatedly expressed its 'strong indignation' to Japan for allowing a conference, entitled 'The

Biggest Lie of the Twentieth Century: Documenting the Rape of Nanking', to proceed on 21 January in Osaka. A right-wing nationalist group, the Society to Correct the Biased Display of War-related Material, organised the conference to dispute the atrocity, claiming that the figure of 140,000 civilian deaths at the hands of Japanese troops over six days in 1937 is 'an exaggeration, if not a total fabrication'. Chinese and western historians put the figure at 300,000 deaths. Osaka city officials refused to halt the conference 'because it would infringe the constitutional right to free speech', while the government, confirming it did not deny the massacre had occurred, said the conference was a matter for the Osaka authorities to decide. Government websites have since been sabotaged by unknown hackers protesting against Japan's stance. On 18 January the Management and Coordination Agency's home page bore the slogan 'Chinese people must speak up to protest the Japanese government for refusing to acknowledge the historical misdeed of the 1937 Nanjing Massacre'. The Science and Technology Agency's home page had a switch implanted taking visitors directly to a pornographic site. A further five attacks over the next two days prompted the government to close the sites and call for an urgent review of security. (Associated Press, Muzi.com, Reuters, *Washington Post*.)

Aum Shinrikyo, the 'doomsday' cult responsible for the poisonous gas attack on Tokyo's subway system in 1995, publicly disassociated itself from their leader and founder, **Shoko**

Asahara on 18 January, saying he was 'likely involved with the series of crimes he is charged with'. He is currently on trial on 16 charges including murder. The cult is going through a process of 'drastic reform', instructing members to abandon 'dangerous dogma' and to present 'no threat to society'. Observers claim the changes are an attempt by the cult's leaders to put themselves beyond the scope of an 'anti-cult' law promulgated in November 1999 (*Index* 1/2000). The cult's name has been changed to Aleph. (*New York Times.*)

KAZAKHSTAN

The editors of the opposition newspaper *XXI Vek* suspended publication between 9 December 1999 and 12 January 2000 because no publishing house in Almaty would print the newspaper. *XXI Vek* has struggled to find printers for several months (*Index* 1/2000). (RFE/RL)

Local independent newspaper *HBC-Press* was suspended from publishing for three months from 25 January after the Ust-Kamennogorsk city court ruled it had published materials 'undermining the independence and sovereignty of Kazakhstan'. The paper's 25 November edition published an appeal by **Viktor Kazimirchuk**, leader of a group of 22 ethnic Russians arrested several days earlier for having allegedly planned to occupy administrative buildings in Ust-Kamennogorsk, capital of East Kazakhstan Oblast, and proclaim an independent Russian Altai Republic. *HBC-Press*'s editor, **Oleg Ablakaev**, was formally

charged with supporting separatism on 27 January. Kazimirchuk has been taken to a psychiatric hospital in Almaty. (RFE/RL)

The offices of the independent newspaper *Edil-Zhayiq* in the town of Oral in western Kazakhstan were broken into on 29 or 30 January. All the newspaper's equipment was destroyed and several documents were stolen. (RFE/RL)

KENYA

Managing editor **Vitalis Musebe** and news editor **Mukalo wa Kwangyera** of the independent *People* newspaper were arrested on 18 January after publishing an article claiming military intelligence had put the armed forces on high alert against possible attacks on military installations, communication centres, hospitals and armouries. Part of the charges against them was an allegation that they had published 'a coded signal meant for the Kenya army'. They have been released on bail pending a reappearance in court on 14 February. (NDIMA, Media Institute)

On 20 January it was reported that exiled Ethiopian journalist **Berhanu Liyew**, arrested outside the offices of the International Organisation for Migration the previous week, was still detained by police. Although he has been taken to court several times since his arrest, the case has not been heard. Berhanu is charged with being in Kenya illegally and failing to produce identification papers. (NDIMA)
On 27 January the newly-

launched Citizen Radio was ordered to cease broadcasting after the recently established Communications Commission of Kenya (CCK) cancelled its frequency licences. The service was broadcast in four regions of the country. The CCK accused parent company Royal Media of shifting one of its transmitters from the authorised location and using unauthorised equipment. The company has been further accused of defaulting on a payment of Ksh10.2 million (approx. US$ 145,798) for the frequencies in 1998 and 1999. Royal Media was one of the first privately run media stations allowed to operate outside of Nairobi. (NDIMA)

KIRIBATI

Two men trying to set up the first non-government owned radio station were fined A$35 each for importing equipment and running a radio station without the appropriate licences. **Ieremia Tabai**, a former Kiribati president, and **Atiera Tetoa**, had been told by a lawyer that they did not need a licence and had also maintained regular contact with the authorities over the station, it was reported on 8 December. The lawyer said Tabai and Tetoa believe that their treatment was 'politically motivated due to the fact that both accused are members of the opposition party'. (PINA)

KUWAIT

Ahmed Zahra, a photographer for the daily *Al-Rai al-Aam*, was brutally beaten on 24 January by recently elected member of parliament Khaled al-Adweh and his supporters in the al-Ahmedi district south of Kuwait City. Sources reported that 'the incident began after Zagra had photographed al-Adweh firing a Kalashnikov rifle in the air during a celebration of his election victory'. Adweh allegedly responded by pointing his firearm at the journalist and then punching him several times. A group of al-Adweh's supporters joined in the attack, knocking the journalist to the ground and punching and kicking him repeatedly. Zahra was treated for his injuries in hospital and released after four hours. (CPJ)

KYRGYZSTAN

At its 14 January sitting the Supreme Court declined to overturn a 200,000 som (US$6,670) fine against the opposition newspaper *Res Publica* for insulting the honour and dignity of Amanbek Karypkulov, president of the National Television and Radio Corporation (*Index* 3/1999, 4/1999, 5/1999). *Res Publica* editor **Zamira Sydykova** said the paper would now appeal to the Constitutional Court. (RFE/RL)

NGOs wrote to the authorities on 28 January protesting that pro-government candidates for the 20 February parliamentary elections had greater access to the media than opposition candidates. Also on 28 January, opposition El (Bei Bechara) Party chairman Daniyar Usmenov, who is being held under arrest in a Bishkek hospital, said he was not allowed to receive visits from prospective voters 'because of a 'flu epidemic currently sweeping the city'. (RFE/RL)

LATVIA

Lilita Grundule, a student testing the country's freedom of information procedures, was harassed by police in Jelgava on the night of 9 December after she filed a request for material on police education, citizens' complaints and juvenile crime statistics on 3 December. A police inspector visited her at home around midnight asking her to appear at the local police station two days later to explain her actions. Officials later said that the material was not secret or restricted and that, if they had known of the survey, they would have provided the information, Grundule explained that the project for Transparency International was to determine the responsiveness of government institutions to requests by ordinary citizens. (*Dienas*)

LEBANON

It was reported on 21 December that the film *A Civilised People* by **Chahal Sabbag**, which won a UNESCO prize at the Venice Film Festival, had 50 minutes of its one hour 41 minutes cut out by the Lebanese government censor (*Index* 1/2000). The film is about the Lebanese civil war and none of Sabbag's previous films about the conflict have been screened in the country. (*Washington Post*)

LIBERIA

Sarkilay Kantan and **Isaac Menyongai**, news editor and reporter for the bi-weekly *Concord Times*, were arrested in Monrovia on 30 December following allegations of 'criminal malevolence' by Alexander Kule,

chief of the National Agency for Refugees. The journalists wrote about racketeering and corruption in government and state-run companies. Warrants were also issued for the arrests of managing editor **Lyndon Ponnie**, editor-in-chief **Sherman Seekuah** and reporters **James King** and **Togba Tuwray**. (RSF)

LITHUANIA

Baltijos Bangu Radijas (Baltic Wave Radio), a new Belarusian language radio station based in Vilnius, launched on 1 January on MW 612 kHz rebroadcasting programmes from Radio Liberty in Prague, Radio Racja in Bialystock, Radio Polonia in Warsaw and Lithuanian Radio in Vilnius. Under editor **Siarhei Shupa**, the private service aims to broadcast uncensored news and programming in Belarusian. (RFE/RL, BAJ)

MALAYSIA

On 14 January it was reported that **Karpal Singh**, defence lawyer for former Deputy Prime Minister Anwar Ibrahim (*Index* 6/1998, 1/1999, 2/1999, 3/1999, 4/1999, 6/1999) and opposition Democratic Action Party (DAP) deputy chairman, was arrested on charges of making seditious remarks while defending Mr Anwar in court. Charging lawyers with sedition for statements made in court in defence of their clients threatens the right of fair trial. (AI, RSF)

A group of leading government critics, journalists and publishers were arrested as part of the government's latest crackdown on those expressing critical views, it was reported on 20 January. **Zulkifli Sulong**, editor of opposition Parti Islamic SeMalaysia newspaper *Haraka* (*Index* 1/2000), and **Chia Lim Thye**, owner of the *Haraka* printing company and holder of the newspaper's publishing licence, were arrested on charges of sedition after an article published on 2 August criticised the government's handling of the trial of former Deputy Prime Minister Anwar Ibrahim. In January the government warned the private newspapers *Haraka, Detik, Wasilah, Tamadun* and *Ekslusif* against spreading 'rumours' and supporting opposition parties and their issues were banned from news stands in a bid to limit sales to part members only. (A19, HRW)

MEXICO

The former editor of the north-eastern daily *El Independiente*, **José Luis Hernández Salas**, had to flee to the USA in September following death threats and alleged attempts by the local state governor to have him removed from the newspaper for political reasons. Sonora state governor Armando López Nogales allegedly used his influence among *El Independiente*'s shareholders and the local courts to push out Hernández, after the editor refused to be bribed into supporting the presidential campaign of López's friend and ruling-party candidate, Francisco Labastida Ochoa. López promised to inject large amounts of money into the paper, if it backed Labastida's campaign. Hernández flatly refused and, on 3 September, representatives of a minority shareholder in *El*

Independiente – La Voz de Sonora – went to the paper's offices with a locksmith. Hernández counter-attacked with a hard-biting editorial and lodged a formal complaint at the local attorney general's office. La Voz de Sonora responded by starting legal proceedings against the editor. On 7 September, 20 police officers led by the local police chief surrounded the *El Independiente*'s offices and Hernández's house. While his house was watched over by police, the journalist received several death threats over the phone. The following day he managed to slip out and escape to the USA with his family, where he still fears for his life. (National Centre for Social Communication)

MOLDOVA

The Chisinau offices of the independent Russian-language daily *Novy Poriadok* (The New Order), which specialises in political investigative reports, were vandalised on the night of 7 January with swastikas and nationalist graffiti such as 'Russian occupants, go home!'. The chairman of the Moldovan Journalists Association, **Valeriu Sahnareanu** claims the publication has 'neo-facist leanings' but would not comment further on the attack until after police investigations. (RSF, REF/RL)

It was reported on 7 January that Russian-language daily *Kommersant Moldova* may face closure by the Prosecutor's General Office for 'using terms' which are supposedly directed against Moldova's statehood. The office claims that the use of terms

such as the 'Transdniester Moldovan Republic' amounts to the propagation of separatism and the implicit recognition of a second state on national territory. (RFE/RL)

NEW ZEALAND

The government has formally admitted to being a member of the global surveillance system Echelon, in collaboration with the US, the UK, Australia and Canada, it was reported on 28 December (*Index* 5/1998). (Global Internet Liberty Campaign)

NIGERIA

Major Adeyi, deputy editor-in-chief of *Tell* magazine in Jos, was arrested on 3 January by members of the State Security Service and taken to Abuja for interrogation. The arrest followed an interview with Senator Joseph Waku, who has called for a military coup to unseat President Olusegun Obasanjo. Waku has since been suspended from the Senate. (IJC)

On 15 January **Uche Maduemesi** of *Tell* magazine in Enugu was assaulted and slapped in the face by the state governor's security guard. The previous day the governor had accused Maduemesi of writing hostile reports about the government. (IJC)

More than 50 police invaded the International Press Centre in Lagos on 20 January. Journalists were threatened, offices ransacked and files taken away. The action follows the use of the centre's conference facilities on the morning of 20 January by the

Oodua Liberation Movement. Police claimed terrorists had been present at the conference. (WAJA)

On 3 February military personnel from Signal barracks, Arakan, interrogated ten journalists visiting land in Ajegunle, a Lagos suburb. The journalists, who were assessing damage done to the shanties and the occupants of Ajegunle, were told they had no right to visit or take photos. (IJC)

NORWAY

On 10 January the board of the non-fiction Writers and Translators Association (NFF) dismissed **Mari Toft**, editor of their magazine *Prosa*. She had recently written a critical report on two Norwegian publishers who had bought the University Press in Norway. One happened to be a close friend of Trond Berg Eriksen, chairman-elect of the NFF. Toft claims that her dismissal came as a result of Eriksen's friendship with the publishers and the fact that he 'wanted [her] out of the way if he was to become chairman'. The NFF said her dismissal was due to the fact that they wanted a 'more politically relevant' magazine and did not feel she was the right person for the job. (*Nyheter*)

PAKISTAN

Nawaz Zulfiqar Memon of the *Daily Nation* died on 16 December after being tortured by law enforcement agents in Islamabad. He was detained on 3 December and tortured for three days at Islamabad airport police station after he had attempted to meet Chief Executive General Pervez Musharraf to seek justice

for an incident on 26 November in his home town, Thatta. Memon had been beaten up after trying to prevent hooligans attacking a school bus driver, but local police refused to register the attack. Memon's father managed to obtain his release and return him home, but he remained unconscious for three days and later died. (PPF)

Hafiz Tahir Khalil of the Urdu-language daily *Jang* was injured while fending off two attackers outside his home in Islamabad on 31 December. The attackers, who lured him over by offering a video on behalf of a former MP, threatened him at gunpoint. They fled before police arrived. (RSF)

PALESTINE

The last detainees arrested by the PNA in November for signing *Manifesto 20* (*Index* 1/2000) were released on 6 January. Professor **Abdul Sattar Qasem** and **Ahmed Shaker Dudeen**, both lecturers at al-Najah university, in Nablus, were held for 40 days. The manifesto, which condemned corruption within the Palestinian leadership, had been signed on 27 November by 20 individuals, including members of the Legislative Council. Qassem was also shot in 1995 after writing an article criticising Arafat. (*Jerusalem Times*)

PANAMA

President Mireya Moscoso signed a bill on 20 December eliminating two of the country's 'gag laws' used to stifle press freedom. Describing them as a 'sword of Damocles hanging over

the media in Panama', Moscoso pledged to work towards eliminating all restrictive press legislation over the next six months. (CPJ)

PERU

The Transport and Communications Ministry ordered the closure on 9 December of Radio Libertad in the northern city of Trujillo, alleging the radio station was operating illegally. According to the station's director-general, **Carlos Burmester**, Radio Libertad has been fully licenced since 1951. Burmester claims to have received a visit days earlier from intelligence agents who warned him to change the independent style of his radio programme *The Voice from the Street*. Opposition congress members have asked for an explanation. (IPYS, IFJ)

The Public Ministry came under fire in December after accepting criminal charges brought by the Supreme Council of Military Justice against the journalists' association, Prensa Libre, for allegedly forging documents implicating the Intelligence Service in harassment campaigns against opposition presidential candidates (*Index* 6/1999). The ministry has since shelved the charges, pending further investigations. (IPYS, IFJ)

Journalists **Henry Vásquez Limo** and **Edgar Valladares Orozco** of the TV news programme *Frecuencia Latina* were allegedly brutally beaten on 18 December by a group of extremist members of the National Solidarity Party in the district of Leonardo Ortíz. They

●●●●●●●●●●●●●●●●●●●●●●●●●●●●●●●●●●

LINUXWORLD
Butterfly on a disc

L inuxWorld: How did you get involved with DVD (Digital Video Disc)?
Jon Johansen: Well, I bought my first DVD-ROM and an MPEG-2 decoder card about two years ago. At the end of September last year, I got in contact with a German computer programmer and a Dutch computer programmer, and we decided that it was time to add DVD support to Linux.

LW: Had you expected any problems when you set about to make the player?

JJ: We knew that they would probably go after someone. But when [Norwegian authorities] visited me yesterday with a search warrant, I really hadn't expected them to, because it's been about two or three months now since [the subject] first appeared in the media and, well, to me, that's a pretty long time.

LW: Did they question you at your house?

JJ: No. They took me to the local police station.

LW: And do you know what is going to happen next?

JJ: They are currently investigating, and I still haven't got my computers back. So I have ordered a new one today, which I will be receiving on Friday. Which is a bit too late, because ABC News is coming tomorrow, and I was supposed to demonstrate DVD playback under Linux.

LW: Why did you decide to come forward and to not remain anonymous?

JJ: I think the first reporter I talked to was from *Wired*, and he asked me if he could publish my name.

LW: Are you sorry now that you did?

JJ: Not really, because I think the fight we are now fighting is a very important fight for free speech and for the open source community.

LW: Why is it so important?

JJ: Basically, if reverse engineering is banned, then a lot of the open source community is doomed to fail. You need to reverse-engineer when creating software for compatibility with, for example, Microsoft Windows. This has nothing to do with copying, which the Copy Control Association and Motion Picture Association of America (MPAA) are claiming.

On 24 January, under pressure from US authorities, Norwegian police arrested 16-year-old computer programmer **Jon Johansen** *for co-developing sofware which allows playback of DVDs on Linux-powered computers, rather than Microsoft and Mac. Citing fears of piracy, the MPAA and others are trying to prevent 'reverse engineering' – analysis and deconstruction – of the encryption software which limits DVD playback. Linux, the emerging rival to Microsoft's computer operating system, is free and development work is chiefly carried out by an army of volunteer coders worldwide. This excerpt is taken from an article published on* **www.linuxworld.com**

●●●●●●●●●●●●●●●●●●●●●●●●●●●●●●●●●●●●

had been preparing to cover the launch of Luis Castañeda Lossio's presidential candidature. (IPYS)

Journalist **Carlos Infante Yupanqui**, who heads the Ayacucho weekly *Democracia*, claims he has been receiving threats and subjected to a smear campaign since publishing a report on irregularities in several local institutions and organisations. The person believed to be behind the threats is local municipality member Melia Luz Quintanilla Melgar. An anonymous pamphlet circulating since 20 December has tried to rake up Infante's supposedly murky past as a terrorist. Although imprisoned between 1992 and 1994 on terrorism charges, Infante was later absolved when it was shown that the charges against him had been fabricated. (IPYS)

Judicial police forced their way into the premises of the new dissident daily *Liberación* on 21 December in an attempt to seize the paper's printing presses. Authorities claimed they were trying to seize assets used as collateral for a bank loan. *Liberación*'s editor, **César Hildebrandt**, accused the government of wanting to take the newspaper out of circulation (*Index* 2/1998, 4/1998, 4/1999, 6/1999). Launched in November, *Liberación* has become one of the strongest critics of President Alberto Fujimori's regime. The newspaper's building is owned by businessman Abraham Hochman Bilbao, who since 1995 has had an outstanding debt with the Bank of Commerce. However, Hochman said he doesn't own the equipment that police tried

to seize. Hilderbrandt remarked it was strange that, only 34 days after the daily's first appearance, a legal case against the premises' owner that had been lying dormant for three years was revived all of a sudden. (IPYS)

A Lima court issued an order on 21 December for the arrest of businessman and former president of the Peruvian Association of Radio and Television **Genaro Delgado Parker**, who has fled to Miami after facing fraud charges. Delgado claims he is being persecuted for having spoken out against the alleged lack of press freedom in television. The businessman is accused of unlawfully appropriating funds while arranging an advertising contract in 1996 for TV company Panamericana Televisión. (IPYS)

Police officers in the Amazonian town of Aucayacu seized video and photographic materials on 23 December from journalists covering an explosion in a local military base that killed five soldiers. According to the daily *La República*, police stripped journalists of their cameras and video recorders, destroying film and video footage. The explosion, reported by authorities as accidental, took place in a counter-insurgency military base. (IPYS)

Caretas weekly journalist, **Horacio Potestá**, received a one-year suspended sentence on 29 December and a US$5,800 fine in a libel suit filed by Javier Corrochano Patrón, a lawyer who has defended drug traffickers in court and is apparently linked to the chief of the intelligence service, Vladimiro Montesinos.

The Fifth Lima Criminal Court ruled that a number of Potestá's articles on Corrochano's alleged criminal activities were unsubstantiated. Potestá alleged that Corrochano had helped a drug trafficker leave the country and been involved in blackmail. Potestá is appealing. (IPYS)

Cameraman **Angel Rojas Montero** was kidnapped on 1 January and threatened with death by an armed assailant in La Perla district of Callao province. The kidnapper, armed with a 9mm pistol, accused the journalist of being a secret police informer. Rojas, who used to work for the cancelled television programme of *Liberación* editor **César Hildebrandt**, was driving his car when the unidentified assailant forced him to stop and jumped in. They ended up driving to a petrol station, where the kidnapper forced him to his knees and threatened to kill him in front of a crowd of bystanders. Despite there being a police station near the petrol station, police did not intervene during the half-hour incident. *Liberación* reported that the short-lived kidnap was meant as a warning to Hildebrandt. (IPYS)

Journalists covering a demonstration in Lima on 6 January against the president's re-election were attacked with rocks, glass bottles and wooden sticks by protesters. Those attacked were reporter **Bayron Horna** and cameraman **Miguel Ascencios** of Canal 2's *Frecuencia Latina* programme; **John Ariza** and **Dany Felipa**, reporter and cameraman respectively of Canal 9's *Andina de Televisión* programme; and **Aldo Kom** of Canal N. (IFJ)

The anti-opposition defamatory tabloid *Repudio* (*Index* 5/1999) reappeared on newsstands on 6 January after three months out of circulation. The tabloid is dedicated to attacking congressman and *La República* daily editor **Gustavo Mohme Llona** – a persistent opponent of Alberto Fujimori's government. Originally launched in May 1999 and copying *La República*'s format and logo, *Repudio* is one of several pro-government pamphlets distributed daily to discredit opposition leaders and independent journalists (*Index* 4/1998, 1/1999, 4/1999, 6/1999) (IPYS)

Interviews with two prominent exiles broadcast on 8 January on journalist **Oscar Díaz**'s political radio programme, *La Revista del Momento*, were publicly condemned two days later by the owner of the programme's radio station, Lima-based Radio Miraflores. Station owner, journalist Ricardo Palma, went on air to blast the interviews with exiled businessman **Baruch Ivcher** and exiled former president **Alan García Pérez**, saying he would not have allowed them on the show if he had known beforehand. (IPYS)

Baruch Ivcher – on a visit to Spain to condemn the allegedly illegal takeover of his television channel, Canal 2, by the Winter brothers – had to flee to Israel on 11 January after Spanish police received orders from Interpol to arrest him. The warrant was posted by the Lima government in connection with a 1998 sentence pending against Ivcher (*Index* 4/1997, 6/1997, 1/1998, 2/1998, 3/1998, 4/1998, 5/1998, 6/1998, 2/1999,

4/1999, 5/1999, 1/2000). The order was issued despite Ivcher being under the protection of the Interamerican Commission on Human Rights for the past year and a half. (IPYS)

The controversial radio news programme *Live News* (*Noticias en Directo*), broadcast via Radio Karibeña in the Amazonian city of Iquitos, was pulled by the station's owners on 17 January against the wishes of its producer and presenter **Fernando Vásquez Barbarán**. Vásquez's bosses felt that the programme was too critical of the government. (IPYS)

Rafael Rey, the vice-presidential candidate of independent opposition party Avancemos, accused the heads of *Frecuencia Latina* (Canal 2), Panamericana Televisión (Canal 5), Andina de Televisión (Canal 9), Global Televisión (Canal 13), Televisión Nacional (Canal 7) and América Televisión (Canal 4) on 25 January of refusing to air the party's political advertisements for the upcoming elections. (IPYS)

RUSSIAN FEDERATION

Aleksandr Nikitin, a Russian engineer charged with high treason and divulging state secrets in June 1999 (*Index* 5/1999), was acquitted in St Petersburg on 29 December at the end of his eighth court appearance. (Bellona Foundation)

It was reported on 3 November that photographs taken by Latvian journalist **Atis Klimovics** were manipulated by the Russian government when one, which depicted the central market in Grozny, was cropped to

prove that a terrorist base in the city had been destroyed. The picture had shown civilians selling food and one individual selling weapons, just a day prior to a Russian rocket attack which killed more than 100 people. In the version that was subsequently used, food stalls were cut out and only the weapons seller was visible. The photographs had been passed to Mikhail Margelov, director of Russian Information Services, by Czech journalist **Petra Prohazkova** to prove that a civilian market had been bombed. (RFE/RL)

Hundreds of journalists and human rights campaigners demonstrated outside the police ministry in Moscow on 28 January after **Aleksandr Khinshteyn,** a television and newspaper journalist who specialises in reporting government sleaze, went into hiding to avoid being taken into to a psychiatric clinic by police who wanted him detained for alleged 'driving offences'. (*Guardian*)

It was reported on 21 January that NTV's co-founder and general director, **Oleg Dobrodeyev,** had left his position over what appear to have been the result of disagreements over policy in the coverage of the Chechen campaign. In recent months Dodrodeyev had appeared deeply depressed by the sharp decline in journalism standards, commenting after the 19 December elections that 'All television channels came out of this election campaign with huge losses to their reputations'. (*Moscow Times*)

SAUDI ARABIA

On 10 January it was reported that three dissident sheikhs, **Safar Hawali**, **Salman Audah** and **Nasser Omar**, jailed since 1994 had been released. They had criticised the corruption of the Saudi monarchy and the alleged lack of strict Islamic codes in the government. (*Washington Post*)

SERBIA-MONTENEGRO

The state-controlled daily *Politika* was charged in late 1999 with libel by **Momcilo Perisic**, who was sacked as head of the Yugoslav Army in 1999. In a published interview with General Nebojsa Pavovic, current head of the Third Yugoslav Army, it was alleged that Perisic had collaborated with the Western Alliance. *Politika* was acquitted on 17 December on the grounds that the report carried a verbatim statement from Pavovic. (ANEM)

The publication of an article entitled 'Requiem without a Patriarch' in the independent daily *Danas* on 18 December prompted accusations from Dussan Djordjevic, director of state press agency Tanjug, that the newspaper had violated Article 69 by 'inciting prejudice against the agency'. The newspaper was fined 150,000 dinars (approx. US$13,370) on 21 January at the end of the first legal case in which one media company sued another. *Danas* has had five fines imposed on it under the Public Information Act since October, including a 60,000 dinar award (approx. US$5,350) against director **Dussab Mitrovic** and editor **Veseljko Koprivica**. Meanwhile, editor-in chief of the

state radio and television publication *Komuna*, **Rajko Popovic**, laid claims for damages against the Kikinda daily *Kikindske Novine* for a story published on 5 November entitled 'Rajko summonsed with force'. The Kikinda magistrate dismissed the charges. Popovic was himself a victim of the Information Act along with **Dragoljub Milanovic**, the general manager of Radio Television Serbia, and were fined for not carrying the name and address of its publisher. The charges followed a complaint by the chairman of the Kikinda Municipality but they were revoked by the Novi Sad Misdemeanours Council on 5 January. (RSF, ANEM)

The unnamed publisher and the editor-in-chief, **Vakasin Obradovic**, of the private daily *Novine Vanjske* were fined 600,000 dinars (US$53,475) and 200,000 dinars respectively on 23 December by Vranske's Correction Tribunal in southern Serbia for violating the 1998 Information Law, following a complaint by the Yugoslav Army. The fines are for the publication of a report by the Helsinki Committee on Human Rights on Albanians who fled Serbia during the NATO bombing under pressure from the police. The army claims the report 'incites religious and racial hatred on a national scale'. (RSF)

Dejan Nebrigic, founder of Arkadija gay rights movement in Serbia, was strangled with a computer wire in his Pancevo apartment between 28-29 December after a lifetime of campaigning against homophobia and all forms of discrimination.

He claimed to be the 'only openly gay man in Serbia' and his apartment had been robbed four times in 1999 for what he believed was 'pure homophobic unruliness'. Arkadija was also part of the Belgrade Peace Movement. (Greek Helsinki Monitor, BETA)

Disciplinary investigations aginst **Zoran Rakic**, the former editor of Television Leskovac, led to his sacking on 29 December after it was revealed that he had been working for other independent media while on sick leave. Rakic aired criticism of the station's editorial policy, refusing to edit programmes or put his name on texts dictated by others. (ANEM)

In an open letter to the management of Radio Television Serbia, editors **Mira Otasevic** and **Bojana Andric** and journalist **Milka Danilovic** left a television project on 13 January in protest at unwarranted censorship of episodes that had already been completed. (ANEM)

Studio B, Serbia's largest non-state broadcaster with more than two million viewers, had vital broadcasting equipment stolen from the transmission tower on Mount Kosmaj site 40 kilometres south of Belgrade on 16 January in what director **Dragan Kojadinovic** believes to be a politically motivated attack. In the last six months several attempts have been made to jam news broadcasts or current affairs programmes: this latest sabotage occurs following the station's installation of anti-jamming equipment and its broadcasting of the political platforms of opposition parties. The lost equipment cannot be replaced in Serbia. (Institute for War and Peace Reporting, Free B92)

Former police officer Dobrosav Gavric was arrested on 22 January for the murder of Zeljko ('Arkan') Raznatovic, the wanted leader of the paramilitary Tigers and criminal, who was shot dead at the Hotel Intercontinental in Belgrade on 15 January. Gavric, who was known to be under the protection of well-known gangsters, and his two accomplices confessed to the attack and will be brought before the Municipal Court. News of the politically significant killing was slow to emerge: state television did not report the story until late in the evening and only in the 30th minute of the evening news. (IWPR, *Guardian*, Free B92)

Nezavisna Svetlost, a daily in the central city of Kragujevac, was fined 100,000 dinars on 28 January over a report on striking school teachers brought by local school headteacher Radmila Paunovic Stajn. She claimed the article damaged her honour and reputation. (ANEM)

Public protests against the 1998 Public Information Law are planned for the last Monday in every month until the act is replaced by legislation in accordance with Article 46 of the Constitution. The first rally, organised by the Independent Association of Serbian Journalists, took place in Belgrade's central Republic Square on 31 January. (Free B92, ANEM)

A computer, valued at 32,000 dinars and containing the entire records of the Kragujevac bureau

of the Belgrade daily *Blic*, was stolen on the night of 29 January following a burglary at the new offices on a central road in the city. (ANEM)

SRI LANKA

On 1 December **A. Sivanesachelvam**, editor of the daily *Thinakkural*, was interrogated by police allegedly for publicising the plight of civilians in the northern Vanni region. (*Sri Lanka Monitor*)

During the presidential election campaign on 16 December, artists campaigning for Ranil Wickremasinghe, the opposition United National Party candidate, were severely assaulted in Gampaha by suspected government activists. (Free Media Movement)

Indika Pathinivasan of Maharaja Television Network (MTV) and **Anura Priynatha Kooray** of Independent Television Network were killed during the attempted assassination of President Chandrika Kumaratunga at her final presidential election rally on 18 December. **K. Karunaratne** and **Shehan Barange** of MTV, **Hiromi Hirose** and **Nobuhiro Ikeda** of Japanese broadcasting company NHK and **Anuruddha Lokuhapuarachchi**, a Reuters photographer, were also injured in the blast. At least 20 people were killed in the attack, which has been blamed on the Liberation Tigers of Tamil Eelam. (CPJ, RSF, *Sunday Times*)

Vasithian Anthony Mariyadasan of the state-run Sri Lanka Broadcasting Corporation was shot dead outside St

Anthony's Church in Vavuniya on 31 December while recording a New Year's Eve midnight mass service for a radio programme. The lone gunman responsible is believed to be a cadre of the Liberation Tigers of Tamil Eelam. (RSF, CPJ, *Sunday Times*)

President Kumaratunga accused independent media of 'ganging up' against her and said such criticism would no longer be tolerated during an address to the nation on 3 January. She named media owners and editors of independent newspapers, threatening to take every possible action 'other than killing' them. The outburst follows a sustained campaign against the independent media by senior ministers, government officials and state-owned media since the president's re-election victory on 21 December. **Lasantha Wickramatunga**, editor of the *Sunday leader*, **Victor Ivan** of *Ravaya* (*Index* 6/1999) and **Waruna Karunatilake**, the convenor of the Free Media Movement (FMM), were top of the Presidential Security Division's (PSD) 'hit list' after President Kumaratunga won a second term, police superintendent Karunaratna told the FMM. The government has acknowledged the PSD's responsibility for the brutal attack on journalists covering an opposition rally on 15 July 1999 (*Index* 5/1999). The PSD is also suspected of murdering *Satana* editor **Rohan Kumara** (*Index* 6/1999). (Free Media Movement, *Sunday Leader*, *Sunday Times*)

Kumar Ponnambalam, the controversial leader of the All Ceylon Tamil Congress, was assassinated on the morning of 5 January after leaving his Colombo home with a Sinhalese man named Shantha. Ponnambalam is believed to have been killed for his increasingly outspoken public support for the Liberation Tigers of Tamil Eelam, who are fighting for a separate Tamil state on the island. On 6 January, a new Sinhalese extremist group called the National Front Against Tigers claimed responsiblity for the murder. (*Sunday Leader, Sunday Times*)

In mid-January allegations emerged in the state media that **Victor Ivan** (*Index* 6/1999), editor of *Ravaya*, and **Lasantha Wickrematunge**, editor of the *Sunday Leader*, were involved in a 'conspiracy' to overthrow the president. Despite the seriousness of these allegations, neither person has been questioned by police. Concerns have been expressed that the accusation of 'conspiracy' is being publicly used as a means to silence criticism of the government. (A19)

TNL Television, which has recently been verbally attacked by the government, charged in late January that its news and political programmes are being jammed. TNL chief **Shan Wickremesinghe** is to complain to the Telecommunications Regulatory Commission that viewers in Hambantota, Ratnapura, Anuradhapura and Nuwara Eliya have reported jamming when the popular political programe *Jana Handa* was being telecast. (*Sunday Times*)

TAJIKISTAN

Three armed masked men attacked **Mukhiddin Idizoda**, deputy editor of the Tajik opposition newspaper *Nadzhot*, near his home on 27 December. The newspaper is funded by the Islamic Renaissance Party. (ITAR-TASS)

TANZANIA

On 14 December the Reverend **Christopher Mtikila**, a religious leader and head of the unregistered Democratic Party, was sentenced to a year in prison for sedition. The case arose in April 1997 when he was accused of uttering defamatory words against the government and leaders of the ruling Chama Cha Mpinduzi (CCM) party. After the death of CCM Secretary-General Horace Kolimba, Mtkila claimed that Kolimba was killed by the ruling party and government. He further equated the CCM leaders to 'Satan'. The presiding judge said Mtikila should be sent to jail although it was his first offence. Mtkila faces other sedition charges in connection with cassettes containing alleged defamatory statements about deceased former president Julius Nyerere (*Index* 1/2000). (MISA)

TOGO

On 23 December **Roland Kpagli Comlan**, editor of the weekly *L'Aurore*, was arrested at his home and taken to the national police station in Lomé. He is accused of publishing an article in the 15 December edition which stated that a secondary-school pupil had been killed by police officers during a clash at a school meeting on 7 December. In fact the girl regained consciousness in hospital. (RSF)

The parliament adopted a press code reform on 4 January which makes provisions for prison sentences with no parole for violation of press laws. Penalties include up to six months' imprisonment and fines of CFA2m (approx US$3,170), notably for cases of 'insulting the head of state'. The bill specifies that 'in the event of a subsequent offence, the maximum two penalties can be applied twofold and consecutively'. The new text also makes provisions for 'the destruction of copies sold, distributed or displayed to the public, and the publication's suspension for a period of one to three months'. In all cases, suspended prison sentences have been abolished. (RSF)

TUNISIA

The office of the publishing house *Edition Aloes*, owned by journalist **Sihem Ben Sedrine**, was twice broken into on 8 and 30 December. Her employees were threatened by members of the security forces. Ben Sedrine is a founder member of the unauthorised National Council for Freedom in Tunisia (CNLT) and a former member of the Tunisian Human Rights League. In the past she has received harassment for her human rights work but the intimidation has increased reportedly due to her intention to start a new independent newspaper. (AI)

On 23 January **Daniel Mermet**, a journalist with France Inter, was detained at the airport on his way back to France. Customs officers confiscated his cassettes and notebooks which contained the addresses of the people he spoke to in Tunisia. (RSF)

TURKEY

The assistant chief of the police intelligence services was found guilty on 6 December of helping to carry out an illegal phone-tapping operation. Zafer Aktas had ordered the destruction of telephone recordings and was sentenced to a six-month jail term. The sentence was immediately commuted to a US$5 fine. (Kurdistan Observer)

Askeri Tan, a young Kurdish singer, was jailed at Diyarbakir Prison on 12 December for having sung in Kurdish at a circumcision celebration for disadvantaged young men. (IMK, Info-Turk)

Police detained 15 members of the Turkish branch of Greenpeace on 21 December at a demonstration against a proposed nuclear power plant at Akkuyu in Mersin. Last year, the nearby city of Adana was struck by a tremor measuring 6.3 on the Richter scale. (Ozgurluk, Agence-France Presse)

The former president of the Human Rights Association of Turkey **Akin Birdal** (*Index* 4/1998, 5/1998, 1/1999, 4/1999, 6/1999, 1/2000) was acquitted on 23 December of aiding the Kurdish guerrilla organisation, the Kurdistan Workers Party (PKK). Birdal, who survived an assassination attempt last year, had been tried on the basis of alleged testimony given by PKK leader Abdullah Ocalan. (Reuters)

The Turkish Appeal Court ruled on 29 December that a university had the right to ban women students from wearing the Islamic headscarf in class. The decision denied the petitioners' appeal for the 'democratic right' to wear a scarf at the University of Samsun. (Kurdistan Observer)

1999 drew to a close in Turkey with few improvements on press freedom: one journalist killed, four tortured, seven jailed, 87 arrested and 26 attacked, with 80 still in prison. In August, under the new Amnesty Law, seven journalists were released, with restrictions on their future activities. (RSF)

Media organisations were warned on 22 January that they could face heavy fines for 'aiding terrorist organisations'. Justice Minister Hikmet Sami Turk proposed that anyone reporting on, or repeating statements, by 'terrorist groups' could be jailed for up to five years. The warning is seen as an attempt to dampen down press enthusiasm for reporting statements that captured Kurdish leader Abdullah Ocalan (*Index* 3/1999, 4/1999) regularly issues from his island jail through his lawyers. Earlier this month, Prime Minister Bulent Ecevit hinted that Ocalan should keep quiet, or they might reverse the decision to await the European Court of Human Rights' ruling on his death sentence. (Reuters)

The burnt and disfigured body of **Konca Kuris**, a radical Islamic feminist and author, was discovered during the January exhumations of dozens of corpses, identified as victims of the extremist Islamic organisation

Hizbullah. Konca Kuris was kidnapped from in front of her home in the town of Mersin in 1998 and disappeared without trace. Her body was found in a shallow grave in Konya and a videotape was recovered containing scenes of torture sessions she had endured over a period of weeks. On one of the tapes, her captors accused her of seeking to become Turkey's version of Salman Rushdie or Talima Nasrin, writers whom some Muslims regard as heretics deserving of death. In her books, articles, lectures and TV appearances, she had described Islam as a positive force for women's rights and asserted that, over the centuries, male commentators had twisted its essence in ways that led to the oppression of women. (*New York Times, Turkish Daily News*)

Nazmi Gur, human rights activist and secretary general of the Human Rights Association of Turkey was charged on 26 January with 'assisting an armed gang organisation', following the publication of an article entitled 'It is not hard to reach peace' on World Peace Day, 1 September. He faces a sentence of up to seven years. (Kurdish Human Rights Project)

The Ankara branch of the Progressive Journalists Union was bombed early on the morning of 28 January. No one was injured, and so far responsibility had not been claimed for the attack. (IFJ)

The Kurdish Foundation for Culture and Research (Kurt-Kav) was cleared at an Istanbul court on 1 February of 'inciting racial hatred' by announcing scholarships for Kurdish-speaking students. The head of the institution faced a jail sentence of up to four and a half years for advertising the scholarships in a daily newspaper. (Agence-France Presse, Kurdistan Observer)

Composer and activist **Sanar Yurdatapan** and journalist **Nevzat Onaran** were sentenced on 1 February to two months' imprisonment for the 38th edition of the bulletin *Freedom of Expression*. In the journal they had expressed their support for woman singer **Nilufer Akbal**, and now-exiled journalist **Koray Duzgoren**. (Cildekt No 159)

The privately owned radio station, Antalya FM was ordered to halt transmission for a year in December after the Supreme Board of Radio and Television judged that it had incited people to terrorism and ethnic hatred. (IFJ)

TURKMENISTAN

Turkmens voted on 12 December in parliamentary elections described by the OSCE as 'inadequate for even a minimally democratic election'. Spurred by the offer of a free watch for all first-time voters, turnout had reached 98.9% even an hour before the polls closed. The newly elected parliament made its first act to name Saparmurat Niyazov president-for-life, despite a 27 December speech in which Niyazov affected to reject the decision. Two days later he told law-makers that no alternatives to the ruling Democratic Party will be allowed to exist during the next decade. (RFE/RL, Interfax)

Two Baptist pastors and their

wives have been forcibly deported from Ashgabat and Turkmenabad, Compass Direct reported on 26 December. **Shagildy Atakov**, a 36-year-old member of the Ashgabat congregation who was forcibly detained on 16 December, was later released. (RFE/RL)

Dissident **Nurberdi Nurmamedov** was detained by ten KGB officers at his home on 5 January after he criticised parliament's decision to extend President Niyazov's term in office indefinitely. Police later charged Nurmamedov with hooliganism and 'making murder threats against a friend', Chariev Amanmeret. Amanmeret denied that any threat was made. On 20 January Nurmamedov's son Murat was placed under house arrest and charged with armed hooliganism. In December Nurmamedov gave three interviews to Radio Liberty's Turkmen Service in which he criticised the parliamentary elections and called the decision of the parliament to effectively make Niayzov president-for-life both anti-democratic and unconstitutional. (Information Centre for Human Rights in Central Asia, HRW, RFE/RL)

The authorities also appear to have begun a campaign to seize the property of exiled writers in early January, occupying the houses of writer **Ewshan Annaqurban** and *Radio Azatlyk* broadcaster **Khudaberdy Hally**. (HRW, RFE/RL)

President Saparmurat Niyazov issued a decree in late January to publish fewer pictures of him in mass media. Among his many accomplishments is to have

founded all Turkmen newspapers except for *Ashgabat*. (*Assa-Irada*)

UNITED KINGDOM

In a letter to the *Daily Telegraph* in early December Iain Banks and other Edinburgh-based writers criticised Edinburgh council and the Scottish Woman's Action Network (SWAN) for using public funds to support a torchlit demonstration followed by a public burning of pornographic books and magazines. The demonstration was part of a larger campaign against violence against women. While supporting that cause, the writers of the letter pointed out that pornography has no proven links to violence against women. (*Daily Telegraph*)

A man convicted of the murder of his occupational therapist won a legal battle with the authorities of Broadmoor Hospital on 12 January when three appeal judges ruled that publication of his book *Armageddon Ahoy* should not be blocked. (*Guardian*)

On 23 December it was reported that charges against **Tony Geraghty**, a journalist accused of breaching the Official Secrets Act by writing a book about the covert activities of the security services in Northern Ireland, have been dropped (*Index* 6/1999). A spokesman for Lord Williams, the attorney general, said that he was no longer 'content' for the case against Geraghty to continue. However the case against **Nigel Wylde**, an army officer and colleague of Geraghty, remains 'under review'. Wylde said the decision to drop charges was designed to limit the publicity that the prosecution would attract. (*Guardian*)

On 13 January the Council of Europe's Committee Against Torture criticised Britain's police, and the Metropolitan Police in particular, for failing to punish officers accused of abuses. It called for the Police Complaints Authority to be replaced by an independent investigation body. (*Daily Telegraph*)

It was reported on 25 January that Labour 'euro-sceptics' accused the BBC of 'outrageous bias' in its coverage of Europe and claimed their views were being ignored by broadcasters 'obsessed' with Conservative splits on the issues. Lord Shore, former Labour cabinet minister and now chairman of the Labour Euro-Safeguards Campaign, noted that the BBC, in line with other major broadcasters, had failed to carry a single interview with a Labour euro-sceptic during 600 hours of coverage for the 1999 European elections. (*Daily Telegraph, The Times*)

Internet service providers in Britain announced new self-regulatory content policies on 25 January aimed at removing racist material from the Internet. The Internet Watch Foundation (IWF), an industry-funded, self-policing body said it will begin cracking down on 'potentially criminal' hate content. The IWF will not recommend prosecution of ISPs if they are doing their best to comply with the law. The organisation originally came into being to remove child pornography from UK administered Web servers, but the government has now asked the IWF to expand their remit. However, Internet Freedom

founder Chris Ellison says the IWF practises 'a form of silent censorship. This material has not been proved to be criminal. The IWF does not refer things to the courts. They just tell ISPs to remove sites and they comply.' (Press Association)

USA

On 9 December President Bill Clinton authorised a law banning 'crush' videos, a new kind of pornographic film which depicts women crushing small animals, such as mice, beneath their heels, often during sex acts. According to police, up to 2,000 'crush' videos are available on the Internet. (Reuters)

On 5 January Laurie Rittenberg, an attorney acting for the city of Los Angeles against the American Civil Liberties Union (ACLU), stated that 'government agencies have the right to regulate the time, place and manner of free speech'. The ACLU had filed a suit on behalf of 'homeless activists'. (*Los Angeles Times*)

On 10 January Pacifica Foundation, parent company of five independent, left-leaning subscription radio stations, completely vacated its premises in Berkeley, California, at night in order to move to a new location in Washington unhindered by protesters. There was national uproar following the sacking of Pacifica Radio's news director on 12 November (*Index* 1/2000). (*Oakland Tribune*)

It was reported on 13 January that a new bill will make it illegal to provide information about drugs on the Internet. The Methamphetamine Anti-

Proliferation Act of 1999 would, for example, make it 'unlawful for any person...to distribute by any means information pertaining to...the manufacture or use of a controlled substance.' Barry Steinhardt of the American Civil Liberties Union said the bill 'will criminalise protected free speech. It would throw in jail persons who merely talk about controlled substances, even when they are describing legal conduct.' (APBnews.com, Global Internet Liberty Campaign)

The government has admitted that workers in nuclear-weapon assembly plants were exposed to radiation which caused cancer and early death. It was reported on 31 January that among workers at 14 such installations there was an unusually high range and rate of cancers. Nearly 600,000 workers have been put at risk since the US began making nuclear weapons at the start of WWII. Energy Secretary Bill Richardson said: 'This is the first time that the government is acknowledging that people got cancer from radiation exposure in the plants.' (*New York Times Service*)

UZBEKISTAN

The Committee to Protect Journalists wrote to President Karimov on 12 January asking him to ensure the release from jail of ailing 63-year-old journalist **Shadi Mardiev**. Mardiev, who worked for the state-run Samarkand radio station, was sentenced in June 1998 to an 11-year prison term on charges of defamation and extortion (*Index* 5/1998, 6/1998). He was arrested in November 1997 after airing a

• •

MAJID TICKLAY
Beyond the frog

A llow me space in your well-read newspaper to make an appeal to the Asian community. To my fellow brothers and sisters whose home is Zambia, I appeal to you to start thinking seriously about the future of this country. Many of us are in our third and fourth generation here.

We have always been law-abiding citizens. We have always worked with the government of the day. But in spite of being loyal citizens, we have always been sidelined because we have sat on the fence for financial and material support. Other than that we are considered as nobody.

The history of Zambia cannot be complete without mentioning the illustrious names of the Kanjombes, the Patels, the Badats, the Desais, the Bobats and the Limbadas. The list is endless about [how] these people helped to liberate this country and assist the government of the day.

It is up to us to now make sure that our children and grandchildren have an identity in the country that we have made our home and this can only be achieved by playing a leading role in the 2001 general elections. Let's stand up and be counted. With our business acumen I am confident we will give a good run to all the political parties.

Our role is to identify which of the political parties we can support. In my own view there are only three parties one could count as opposition to each other. These are UNIP, MMD and UPND.

In 1991 all of us wanted a change, even if we had a frog as a candidate we would have chosen a frog. This time round the story is different. Let's help the people of Zambia choose a party that will help us come out of our present crisis where we have been made destitutes in our own country. ❑

On 28 December, the Post *published a letter from* **Majid Ticklay***, a British Asian resident in Zambia for half a century. Ticklay called for greater involvement by Zambia's Asian community in the electoral process. On 4 January, Minister of Home Affairs Peter Machungwa announced in a press statement that Ticklay had been deported for 'sowing messages designed to promote ethnic divisions, hatred, racial discrimination and anarchy among the people of this country'*

• •

programme implicating a Samarkand prosecutor in corruption. (RFE/RL)

Reports in mid-January indicated that the Interagency Coordination Commission (MKK) decided on 17 November to close two non-governmental TV stations – ALC in Urgench and Aloka A.K. in Gulistan – for failing to renew their licences. Both stations had in fact submitted their renewals in good time. Five other non-governmental stations have continued to broadcast despite the expiration of their licences. (IFJ)

Exiled Uzbek opposition leaders, including the leaderships of the Erk party and Birlik movement, issued a cautious welcome on 26 January to a 22 January call by President Islam Karimov for them to return home. The exiles stipulated that, before they could return, Karimov must meet a number of minimum conditions, including the unbanning of opposition parties and the release of prisoners of conscience. (*Turkistan Newsletter*)

ZAMBIA

Mukalya Nampito-Mwangala, news editor of the *Post* newspaper, was cleared of charges of espionage on 25 November. However the other 11 journalists (*Index* 3/1999) arrested with Nampito-Mwangala remain on trial. (MISA)

Two female reporters were assaulted by police on 17 January while covering a demonstration by women's rights activists in Lusaka against police inertia in an ongoing child rape and murder

investigation. **Rachiel Chiumya** of Radio Phoenix and **Kangwa Mulenga** of *Monitor* newspaper were physically attacked and forced to hand over a recorder and notebooks after they attempted to interview the protesters. They were saved from further injury by the intervention of police spokesperson Lemmy Kajoba and human rights activist Alfred Zulu. (MISA)

On 2 February **David Simpson** of the Zambia Independent Media Association (ZIMA) and **Ngandi Mwanajiti** of the Inter-African Network for Human Rights and Development (AFRONET) were accused of 'betrayal' and of being 'agents of foreign sponsors' by Newstead Zimba, Minister of Information and Broadcasting Services. He also threatened to take 'drastic action' against them. The attack followed claims by the two NGOs that Zimba's ministry had influenced Radio Phoenix to cancel the phone-in programme *Let the People Talk*, sponsored by AFRONET, which focused on a strike by health workers and the subsequent dismissal of junior doctors in Lusaka and Kitwe. The programme was later reinstated. (MISA)

ZIMBABWE

The persecution of journalist **Ray Choto** (*Index* 6/1999, 4/1999, 3/1999) continues. On 29 November an unsigned letter delivered to his office informed him he was being trailed and gave his exact movements on a previous day with a warning he was to be shot. His wife Girlie also received a threatening letter on 1 December at the Choto home. Both Choto and fellow

Sunday Standard journalist **Mark Chavunduka** will have to wait until July for their trial for causing 'alarm and despondency'. President Mugabe recently stated that if the journalists wrote another 'lie' then he will not 'condemn my army for having done that [violent retribution] when they are provoked'. Mugabe also claimed the injuries sustained by the journalists stemmed from a car crash and not from torture. (MISA, CPJ)

Compiled by: Jake Barnes, Shifa Rahman, Daniel Rogers, François Vinsot (Africa); Ruper Clayton, Heidi Joyce, Andrew Kendle, Josie Kirby (Asia); William Escofet, Daniel Rogers (south and central America); Arif Azad, Gill Newsham, Neil Sammonds (Middle East); Humfrey Hunter (north America and Pacific); Steve Donachie (UK and western Europe); Katy Sheppard (eastern Europe and the Balkans)

NORMAN FINKELSTEIN

The Holocaust industry

UK historian David Irving claims that the Jewish 'Holocaust industry' silences its critics by a combination of intellectual terrorism and moral blackmail and he has taken some of his opponents to court to attempt to prove it. It seems he may have some persuasive arguments on his side

'Holocaust awareness,' the Israeli writer Boas Evron observes, is actually 'an official, propagandistic indoctrination, a churning out of slogans and a false view of the world, the real aim of which is not at all an understanding of the past, but a manipulation of the present.'

Two central dogmas underpin the Holocaust framework: the Holocaust marks a categorically unique historical event and the climax of an irrational Gentile hatred of Jews. Although they became the centrepieces of Holocaust literature, neither figures at all in genuine scholarship on the Nazi Holocaust. On the other hand, both dogmas draw on important strands in Judaism and in Zionism.

The 'Holocaust uniqueness' dogma became, according to Peter Novick, author of *The Holocaust in American Life* 'axiomatic', a 'fetishism' and a 'cult' in 'official Jewish discourse'. No speech crime loomed larger than the use of the words 'Holocaust' and 'genocide' to describe other catastrophes. In an illuminating essay, historian David Stannard ridicules the 'small industry of Holocaust hagiographers arguing for the uniqueness of the Jewish experience with all the energy and ingenuity of theological zealots'.

The uniqueness dogma makes no sense. Every historical event is unique, if merely by virtue of time and location, and every historical event bears distinct features as well as features in common with other historical events. The anomaly of the Holocaust is that its uniqueness is held to be crucial. What other historical event, one might ask, is framed largely for its categorical uniqueness? Typically, distinctive features of the Holocaust are isolated in order to place the event itself in a category apart. Novick dismisses this 'gerrymandering' technique as 'intellectual sleight of hand' which entails 'deliberately singling out one or more distinctive features of the event and trivialising or sweeping under the rug those features it shares with other events to which it might be compared'.

All Holocaust writers agree that the Holocaust is unique, but few, if any, agree why. Each time an argument for Holocaust uniqueness is empirically refuted, a new argument is adduced in its stead. The result, according to Jean-Michel Chaumont, is multiple, conflicting arguments that annul each other: 'Knowledge does not accumulate. Rather, to improve on the former argument, each new one starts from zero.' In other words, uniqueness is a given in the Holocaust framework; proving it is the appointed task, and disproving it is equivalent to Holocaust denial. Perhaps the problem lies with the premise, not the proof. Even if the Holocaust were unique, what difference would it make? How would it change our understanding if the Holocaust were not the first but the fourth or fifth in a line of comparable catastrophes?

The most recent entry into the Holocaust uniqueness sweepstakes is Stephen Katz's *The Holocaust in Historical Context*. Citing nearly 5,000 titles in the first of a projected three-volume study, Katz surveys the full sweep of human history in order to prove that 'the Holocaust is phenomenologically unique by virtue of the fact that never before has a state set out, as a matter of intentional principle and actualised policy, to annihilate physically every man, woman and child belonging to a specific people'. His argument is that an historical event containing a distinct feature is a distinct historical event.

Only a flea's hop separates the claim of Holocaust uniqueness from the claim that the Holocaust cannot be rationally apprehended. If the Holocaust is unprecedented in history, it must stand above, and hence cannot be grasped by, history: it is unique because it is inexplicable and inexplicable because it is unique.

Dubbed by Novick the 'sacralisation of the Holocaust', this mystifications's most practised purveyor is Elie Wiesel. For Wiesel, Novick observes, the Holocaust is effectively a 'mystery' religion: it

Baku, 1904. An Armenian lies murdered in the street as normal
life goes on around him – Credit: Camera Press

'leads into darkness', 'negates all answers', 'lies outside, if not beyond, history', 'defies both knowledge and description', 'cannot be explained nor visualised', is 'never to be comprehended or transmitted', marks a 'destruction of history' and a 'mutation on a cosmic scale'. Only the survivor-priest (read Wiesel) is qualified to divine its mystery. 'Any

survivor,' according to Wiesel, 'has more to say than all the historians combined about what happened.' And yet, the Holocaust's mystery, Wiesel avows, is 'noncommunicable'. 'We cannot even talk about it.'

Rationally comprehending the Holocaust means denying it since reason denies the Holocaust's uniqueness and mystery. To desacralise or demystify the Holocaust is accordingly, for Wiesel, a subtle form of anti-Semitism. To compare the Holocaust with the sufferings of others constitutes a 'total betrayal of Jewish history'. Some years back, the spoof of a New York tabloid was headlined, 'Michael Jackson, 60 Million Others, Die in Nuclear Holocaust'. The letters page carried an irate protest from Wiesel: 'How dare people refer to what happened yesterday as a Holocaust? There was only one Holocaust.' The scholarly consensus is that the Holocaust uniqueness debate is sterile. The claims of Holocaust uniqueness have come to constitute a form of 'intellectual terrorism'.

A subtext of the Holocaust uniqueness claim is that the Holocaust was uniquely evil. However terrible, the suffering of others simply does not compare. Proponents of Holocaust uniqueness typically disclaim this implication, but Novick rightly dismisses such demurrals as disingenuous. 'The claim that the assertion of the Holocaust's uniqueness is *not* a form of invidious comparison produces systematic doubletalk ... Does anyone ... believe that the claim of uniqueness is anything other than a claim for preeminence?' (Emphasis in original.)

There is another factor at work. The claim of Holocaust uniqueness is a claim for Jewish uniqueness. Not the suffering of Jews but that Jews suffered is what made the Holocaust unique: the Holocaust is special because Jews are special. Thus Ismar Schorsch, chancellor of Jewish Theological Seminary, ridicules the Holocaust uniqueness claim as 'a distasteful secular version of chosenness'.

For Anti Defamation League (ADL) head Abraham Foxman, the Holocaust 'was not simply one example of genocide but a near successful attempt on the life of God's chosen children and, thus, on God himself'. And Elie Wiesel is no less vehement that Jews are unique than he is about the uniqueness of the Holocaust: 'Everything about us is different.'

The Holocaust dogma of Gentile hatred also validates the complementary dogma of uniqueness. If the Holocaust marked the climax of a millennial Gentile hatred of the Jews, the persecution of non-Jews in the Holocaust was merely accidental and the persecution of non-Jews in history merely episodic. From every standpoint, Jewish suffering during the Holocaust was unique.

Embedded in the Holocaust framework, much of the literature on Hitler's final solution is worthless as scholarship. The first major Holocaust hoax was *The Painted Bird* by Polish emigré Jerzy Kosinski. The book was 'written in English', Kosinski explained, so that 'I could write dispassionately, free from the emotional connotation one's native language always contains'. In fact, whatever parts he actually authored (an unresolved question) were written in Polish. The book purports to be the autobiographical account of a solitary child wandering through rural Poland during WWII. In fact, Kosinski lived with his parents throughout the war. The book's motif is the sadistic, sexual tortures perpetrated by the Polish peasantry. Pre-publication readers derided it as a 'pornography of violence' and 'the product of a mind obsessed with sadomasochistic violence'. The book depicts the Polish peasants he lived with as virulently anti-Semitic. 'Beat the Jews,' they jeer. 'Beat the bastards.' In fact, Polish peasants harboured the Kosinski family, fully aware of their Jewishness and the dire consequences they themselves faced if caught. Kosinski invented most of the pathological episodes he narrates.

In the *New York Times Book Review*, Wiesel acclaimed *The Painted Bird* as one of the best indictments of the Nazi era, 'written with deep sincerity and sensitivity'. Cynthia Ozick later said that she immediately recognized Kosinski's authenticity as 'a Jewish survivor and witness to the Holocaust'. Long after Kosinski was exposed as a consummate literary hoaxer, Wiesel continued to heap encomiums on his 'remarkable body of work'. Best-seller and award-winner, translated into numerous languages, required reading in high school and college classes, *The Painted Bird* became a basic Holocaust text. Finally exposed by an investigative news weekly, Kosinski was still stoutly defended by the *New York Times*, which alleged that he was the victim of a communist plot.

To his credit, Kosinski did undergo a kind of deathbed conversion. In the few years between his exposure and his suicide, he deplored the Holocaust's exclusion of non-Jewish victims. 'Many North American Jews tend to perceive the Shoah as an exclusively Jewish disaster ... But at least half the world's Romanies (unfairly called Gypsies), some 2.5 million Polish Catholics, millions of Soviet citizens and various nationalities, were also victims of this genocide.' He also paid tribute to the bravery of the Poles who sheltered him during the Holocaust despite his so-called Semitic looks. Angrily asked at a Holocaust conference what did the Poles do to save the Jews, Kosinski snapped back, 'What did the Jews do to save the Poles?'

The more recent fraud, Binjamin Wilkomirski's *Fragments*, borrows promiscuously from the Holocaust *kitsch* of *The Painted Bird*. Like Kosinski, Wilkomirski portrays himself as a solitary child survivor who becomes mute, winds up in an orphanage and only belatedly discovers he is Jewish. Like *The Painted Bird*, the chief narrative conceit of *Fragments* is the simple, pared-down voice of a child-naif that allows time-frames and place names to remain vague. Like *The Painted Bird*, each chapter of *Fragments* climaxes in an orgy of violence. Kosinski represented *The Painted Bird* as 'the slow unfreezing of the mind'; Wilkomirski represents *Fragments* as 'recovered memory'. It is the archetypal Holocaust memoir. Every concentration camp guard is a crazed, sadistic monster joyfully cracking the skulls of Jewish newborns.

Yet, the classic memoirs of the Nazi camps concur with the views of
Auschwitz survivor Dr Ella Lingens-Reiner: 'There were few sadists.
Not more than five or ten per cent.' However, ubiquitous German
sadism figures prominently in Holocaust literature.

Yet the singularity of *Fragments* lies in its depiction of life not during
but after the Holocaust. Adopted by a Swiss family, little Binyamin
endures yet new torments. He is trapped in a world of Holocaust
deniers. 'Forget it – it's a bad dream,' his mother screams. 'It was only a
bad dream ... You're not to think about it any more.' 'Here in this
country,' he chafes, 'everyone keeps saying I'm to forget and that it never
happened, I only dreamed it. But they know all about it!'

Driven to abject despair, Binyamin reaches a Holocaust epiphany.
'The camp's still there – just hidden and well disguised. They've taken
off their uniforms and dressed themselves up in nice clothes so as not to
be recognized ... Just give them the gentlest of hints that maybe, possibly,
you're a Jew, and you'll feel it: these are the same people, and I'm sure of
it. They can still kill, even out of uniform.'

Translated into a dozen languages, winner of the Jewish National
Book Award, the Jewish Quarterly Prize, and the *Prix de Mémoire de la
Shoah*, *Fragments* was widely hailed as a classic of Holocaust literature.
Star of documentaries, keynoter at Holocaust conferences and seminars,
fund-raiser for the United States Holocaust Memorial Museum,
Wilkomirski quickly became a Holocaust poster boy.

Acclaiming *Fragments* a 'small masterpiece', Daniel Goldhagen,
author of the controversial 1996 publication *Hitler's Willing Executioners*,
was Wilkomirski's main academic champion. Knowledgeable historians
like Raul Hilberg, however, early on pegged *Fragments* as a fraud.
Wilkomirski, it turns out, spent the entire war in Switzerland. He is not
even Jewish. But Israel Gutman, a former inmate of Auschwitz and now
a director of Yad Vashem and a Holocaust lecturer at Hebrew University,
says it's not that important whether *Fragments* is a fraud. 'Wilkomirski has
written a story which he has experienced deeply; that's for sure ... He is
not a fake. He is someone who lives this story very deeply in his soul.
The pain is authentic.'

The *New Yorker* called its exposé of the Wilkomirski fraud 'Stealing
the Holocaust'. Yesterday Wilkomirski was feted for his tales of Gentile
evil; today he is chastised as yet another evil Gentile. It's always the
Gentiles' fault. True, Wilkomirski fabricated his Holocaust past, but the

larger truth is that the Holocaust industry fabricated Wilkomirski: he
was a Holocaust survivor just waiting to be discovered.

Consider now Holocaust secondary literature. Novick justly describes
Yehuda Bauer, lecturer at the Hebrew University and a director of Yad
Vashem, as a 'leading Israeli Holocaust scholar'. He quotes an article by
Bauer to refute the Goldhagen thesis of German complicity in Hitler's
final solution: 'The Jews were murdered by people who, to a large
degree, did not actually hate them ... The Germans did not have to hate
the Jews in order to kill them.' Yet, in a review of Goldhagen's book,
Bauer maintained the exact opposite: 'The most radical type of
murderous attitudes dominated from the end of the 1930s onward ...
[B]y the outbreak of World War II the vast majority of Germans had
identified with the regime and its antisemitic policies to such an extent
that it was easy to recruit the murderers.' Questioned about this
discrepancy, Bauer replied: 'I cannot see any contradiction between these
statements.'

In the wake of Israel's ill-fated invasion of Lebanon in 1982 and as
official Israeli propaganda claims came under withering attack by Israel's
'new historians' (*Index* 3/1995), apologists desperately sought to tar the
Arabs with Nazism. The historian Bernard Lewis managed to devote a
full chapter of his short history of anti-Semitism, and fully three pages of
his 'brief history of the last 2,000 years' of the Middle East, to Arab
Nazism. *New Republic* literary editor Leon Wieseltier claimed that 'the
Palestinians, or many of them, were Hitler's little helpers in the Middle
East'. According to Novick, Middle East politics are no longer a prime
mover of the Holocaust industry. He quotes a statement by ADL's
Foxman deploring 'the use of Holocaust imagery' in the context of the
Arab-Israeli conflict.

The most recent Holocaust extravaganza is *Hitler's Willing
Executioners*. Every important journal of opinion printed one or more
reviews within weeks of its release. The *New York Times* featured
multiple notices, acclaiming Goldhagen's book as 'one of those rare new
works that merit the appellation landmark'. With sales of half a million
copies and translations slated for 13 languages, *Time* magazine hailed
Hitler's Willing Executioners as the 'most talked about' and second-best
non-fiction book of the year.

Pointing to the 'remarkable research', and 'wealth of proof ... with
overwhelming support of documents and facts', Wiesel heralded the

book as a 'tremendous contribution to the understanding and teaching of the Holocaust'. Gutman praised it for 'raising anew clearly central questions' which 'the main body of Holocaust scholarship' ignores. Nominated for the Holocaust chair at Harvard University, paired with Wiesel in the national media, Goldhagen quickly became a ubiquitous presence on the Holocaust circuit.

The central thesis of Goldhagen's book is standard Holocaust dogma: driven by a pathological hatred, the German people leapt at the opportunity Hitler gave them to murder the Jews. Although disguised as an academic study, *Hitler's Willing Executioners* amounts to little more than a compendium of sadistic violence.

Yet despite the hype, there is no evidence, says Novick, that 'Holocaust deniers' exert the slightest influence in the US. Indeed, given the nonsense churned out daily by the Holocaust industry, the wonder is there are so few sceptics.

The motive behind the claim that there is widespread Holocaust denial is not hard to find. In a society saturated with the Holocaust, how else to justify yet more museums, books, curricula, films and programmes except by conjuring up the bogey of Holocaust denial? Thus Deborah Lipstadt's acclaimed book, *Denying the Holocaust*, as well as a contrived poll alleging pervasive Holocaust denial, were released just as the Washington Holocaust Museum opened.

Denying the Holocaust is an updated version of the 'new anti-Semitism' tracts. To document widespread Holocaust denial, Lipstadt cites publications by – in Novick's words – 'a tiny band of cranks, kooks and misfits'. Her pièce de résistance is Arthur Butz, the protagonist of her chapter 'Entering the mainstream'. Butz, who teaches electrical engineering at Northwestern University, published his book *The Hoax of the Twentieth Century* with a crackpot press; were it not for the likes of Lipstadt, no one would have heard of him

The one truly mainstream holocaust denier is Bernard Lewis. A French court even convicted Lewis of denying genocide. But this was the Armenian genocide and Lewis is pro-Israel. Accordingly, this holocaust denial raises no hackles in the US; the fact that Turkey is an Israeli ally was a further extenuationg circumstance. Mention of the Armenian genocide is, therefore, taboo. Wiesel, Harvard Law School professor Alan Dershowitz and Rabbi Arthur Hertzberg withdrew from an international conference on genocide in Tel Aviv because the sponsors, against government urging, included sessions on the Armenian case. Acting at Israel's behest, the US Holocaust Council 'virtually effaced' mention of the Armenians in the Washington Holocaust Museum; and Jewish lobbyists in Congress blocked a day of remembrance for the Armenian genocide.

To question a survivor's testimony, to denounce the role of Jewish collaborators, to suggest that Germans suffered during the bombing of Dresden or any state except Germany committed crimes in WWII is, according to Lipstadt, all evidence of Holocaust denial. But the most 'insidious' form of Holocaust denial, she suggests, is 'immoral equivalencies': that is, denying the uniqueness of the Holocaust. This argument has intriguing implications. Goldhagen argues that Serbian 'deeds' in Kosovo 'are, in their essence, different from those of Nazi Germany only in scale'. That would make Goldhagen 'in essence' a Holocaust denier. Across the political spectrum, Israeli commentators compared Serbia's 'deeds' in Kosovo with Israeli 'deeds' in 1948 against the Palestinians. Reckoning, then, by Goldhagen, Israel committed a holocaust. Not even Palestinians claim that any more.

Newspaper editors display 'fragility of reason', in Lipstadt's view, if they run a Holocaust denial 'ad or op-ed column that, according to their *own* evaluation, is totally lacking in relevance or substance'. But not all revisionist literature is totally worthless. Lipstadt brands UK historian David Irving 'one of the most dangerous spokespersons for Holocaust denial', yet Irving has also made indispensable contributions towards explaining Nazism. And Arno Mayer, in his important study of the Nazi Holocaust, as well as Raul Hilberg, cite Holocaust denial publications. 'Even if the world is in the right,' Mill wrote in his essay 'On Liberty', 'it is always probable that dissentients have something worth hearing to say for themselves, and that truth would lose something by their silence.' ❏

Norman Finkelstein *teaches political theory at the City University of New York. He is the author of* A Nation on Trial: The Goldhagen Thesis and Historical Truth *(with Ruth Bettina Birn). His latest book,* The Holocaust Industry, *will be published in July by Verso*

Eastern Europe: racism across borders

Austria is not the only European
country where racism and xenophobia
are at the heart of government. In
Poland, the Czech Republic and
Hungary, the eager first wave of
European enlargement, they are
commonplace and – almost –
respectable. As in Russia,
we ignore them at our peril

File compiled by Irena Maryniak

LUDVIK VACULIK

I don't like the look of you, stranger!

There I was just walking down the street in Karlín when I met two men coming the other way. Karlín is a working-class district of Prague where all sorts of odd ethnic groups have started to settle now that peoples are mingling more. The two men were powerfully built and dressed in a repulsive combination of fabric and artificial leather and bedecked with various chains, rings and buckles. Hands in pockets.

They were walking a couple of metres apart, so I could have passed between them, but I didn't dare so gave them a wide berth. Their complexion was somewhat darker than is customary in old Karlín. They were obviously foreigners. Their faces bore no trace of any intellect, they were simply biological: eyes, nose, a mouth devoid of any expression. I could tell they were criminals. And if they weren't, why did they look like that? It's their fault!

It's a fact, I thought to myself, people who look like villains tend to be villains. Mind you, I'm not saying every villain looks like one! There are intelligent, courteous, well-educated villains. I expect these were their henchmen. I turned and followed them with my eyes: they went into a pub. I hurried away before the shooting broke out. But nothing happened and I conceded that they really might just have gone for a pint. I walked on and did some heart-searching. I had to admit that I'd probably kick out people like those two, simply because they look like pals of theirs who've already been caught. Is it right for first offenders to be given a second chance when their first crime is always committed at the expense of one of us?

Mistrust of foreigners – particularly when they look different from us – is natural. From observing dogs in the street it's my feeling they are the only ones oblivious to differences such as size, colour or breed. The sense of smell would seem to be the crucial element in their friendships. The same goes for us, though I'm bound to say from my own experience that first impressions tend to be justified. It's the business of foreigners to assuage our mistrust of them. That's the natural course of things; relying on the theory of universal equality is superficial, self-indulgent and a cop-out. Equality has to be merited: I don't want to be on a par with my potential murderer! So it's up to foreigners to win our trust and we have to be receptive to every sign of goodwill on their part. And it's up to us to try to understand the differences and, when misapprehensions occur, to look for other, more favourable explanations than our snap judgments. Anyway, in my opinion, we are only too happy to abandon our mistrust of foreigners, at which point we tend to be demonstratively friendly and co-operative. And then we feel ashamed at the bad treatment our nice foreigners receive at the hands of others.

I was a young man when Negroes first arrived on the scene in Prague after the war. I regarded them as illustrations of what I'd read about Africa and they all looked alike to me. It took me a time to make out the differences. Personalities began to emerge from the common racial features. The same was later true of the Vietnamese and their ilk. Now we can distinguish between cheerful and miserable people, tell the clever and the stupid, the coarse and the gentle, the honest and the crafty apart. I notice them and enjoy observing them.

But Arabs always have the look of the spiv about them – though I freely admit that it could just be a quirk of mine. It's because when someone here dresses up as an Arab or even an exotic Spaniard, they tend to look a bit like a spiv or some sort of braggart. That long thin moustache – watch out, an obvious gigolo! I don't like foreigners of any race when they flock together at certain spots such as the bottom end of Wenceslas Square. I'd pack the whole lot of them off to the nearest frontier – along with home-made individuals of the same ilk. The gypsies are a different matter entirely: they are one of us – it's an old story. It's a problem that can only be solved on an individual basis. Nevertheless, though it has been politicised recently, I myself see it as more of a social issue than a question of race.

However, my racial researches have come to a rather disagreeable conclusion of late: we whites are the ugliest race of all. Notice how Asians' faces are finer and more delicate. Even in old age there is a liveliness about them, whereas we look debauched and dissipated. From a certain age, our faces start to lose their aesthetic qualities and start to resemble a bad painting. Friends, a race like that isn't worth exporting. But it's too late for a ban – it has long since ruined the entire planet. ❏

Ludvík Vaculík is a Czech journalist and novelist. He was a leading opponent of the Communist regime. His novel The Axe *was a seminal work of the Prague Spring in 1968. His work was banned throughout the 1970s and 80s during which time he devoted himself to publishing his own work and that of other banned authors in his samizdat edition Padlock Books. He continues his critical, often satirical, comments on life at home and abroad.*
Translated by Gerald Turner

ANATOLII PRISTAVKIN

Not one of us

Russia defines itself more by what it is not, than what it is. Fall on the wrong side of that boundary and exclusion can be total

I have never recalled this incident until now. During the war, my father came back from the front to see me at the special children's home in Kizlyar in the Caucasus, and my life changed dramatically. Until then I had been hanging around, making a bit in the market, sometimes begging, sometimes thieving, but now I suddenly grew in self-respect. I had a father, a front-line soldier: I had someone who was going to look after me for the rest of my life.

My friend and classmate Vitya Yoffe lived with his mother in a house on the outskirts of town. Vitya's mother was an accountant at a power station and, despite my scruffiness (at least I didn't have lice), would invite me in and even give me something to eat. Vitya's father, she said, was a pilot who had been killed in the war. At the time I didn't doubt she was telling the truth, but it occurs to me now she must have been making it up. In the photographs hanging on their walls, Vitya's young, curly-haired, bespectacled father looked more like a scholar than a pilot. Nobody ever told me anything about him, so I imagine he must have been one of those 'repressed' by the state who died in the labour camps. Now I was off home, back to Moscow, completely forgetting my friends, and when Vitya asked when I was leaving, I thoughtlessly repeated my father's remark that he might be in trouble if he was late getting back to Moscow because of me, as the director of his factory was a Jew. Even now I remember every detail of that conversation, and Vitya looking down and saying quietly, 'Why, don't you think Jews have human feelings too?'

I think I was very surprised. It had never occurred to me that Vitya was Jewish. Besides, what did it matter what kind of director my father had, when Vitya was my trusted friend. That was what mattered. My friend Khristik was Armenian, and Balbek was a Nagay, and Lida

Zherebnenko was Ukrainian, and that girl Gross was German. But I had had to blab my mouth off, and still hadn't been forgiven by Vitya when I left. I wonder where he is now.

As I remember this today, I feel ashamed. Of course, I said something stupid because of the good fortune that had unexpectedly befallen me, but the fact that I remember it in such detail indicates that I must already then have understood I had done something wrong. And for the next fifty years I had been repressing it, trying not to remember.

What interests me now is something different: from what age do we develop this neanderthal dislike, irritation and hostility towards people of a different tribe or faith, or origin? From childhood? From birth? Or perhaps that is not it, and what I really want to know is how it comes to be there in a person at all. I had a friend in Yalta, that pearl of the Crimea. He was a Jew and his wife was Chinese. He was a talented designer but persecuted by the authorities. Late in life he emigrated to Germany, and now lives in Berlin on a state pension and has few complaints. Except that he has moved to a different part of Berlin twice because he can't stand having 'blacks', that is, Turks, as neighbours. He heatedly told me when we met what a bunch of so-and-sos they all were. 'And what about you?' I was tempted to ask, but didn't. I was disappointed. A slave who overnight ceases to be a slave but retains the mind of a slave is, I have discovered, even more of a slave, and may well go from being the persecuted to being the persecutor.

In my novella *Nochevala tuchka zolotaya* (*The Inseparable Twins*), the teacher in a children's home tells her pupils, 'There are no bad peoples, only bad people.' In the story she is talking about the Chechens who at that time, in 1944, were being called bandits and deported from the Caucasus at the behest of Stalin and Beria. We orphans of the war living in the Moscow region were evacuated by the will of the same leaders to the Caucasus in order to populate and colonise this newly created no-man's-land. We knew little of what was going on, but we had certainly heard many times that the Chechens were enemies who went around killing everybody. For 40 years I carried this theme within me, deeply nervous of dealing with it. My heroes in the novella are children, one Chechen, the other Russian: Alkhuzur and Kolya suffer equally from violence and, meeting in the mountains, the two persecuted outcasts become brothers; because all the people on this earth are brothers.

Recently, in a handwritten mannuscript I came across a passage which read: 'The golden clouds have been blown far away, once more the azure skies over the Caucasus are black. Where are you now my friends, Kolya and Alkhuzur! How great today is the need of your Caucasus for words of courage to silence the guns.' More than half a century has passed, my heroes have grown up, and yet today we are again being told that all the people of Chechnya are bandits and terrorists. It would be bad enough if these were the thoughts of benighted, ignorant people, but this is being proclaimed by renowned writers: Vasily Aksenov, who lives in the USA, and Alexander Solzhenitsyn. Both in their time were persecuted and exiled by the KGB, but those days are past and today Aksenov has it in him to say of his persecutors that those former generals of the Cheka are now worthily performing their duty towards Russia by imposing their iron order on Chechnya.

The notion of Russia's national interest, which has always been seen as opposed to progress as a movement in the direction of the West and its democracy, has slowly but surely been gaining ground with the masses, not without the connivance of our unprincipled and corrupt press. Here we again find the whole familiar gamut of slogans about the national ideal, about American imperialism, the special path to be followed by Russia and, of course, about criminal peoples bent on bringing about the disintegration of Russia. Even Aushev, the president of Ingushetia, has been declared an enemy. That figure 'a person of Caucasian nationality' keeps cropping up in criminal investigations although, according to calculations made by the late Bulat Okudzhava, natives of the Caucasus actually represent a very modest proportion of criminals in Russia, a fraction of one per cent. And yet, even when a criminal is unknown, it will be officially noted that 'no sign of Chechen involvement has so far been discovered'. Why not Bashkir involvement? Or Kalmyk? Simply because it is obvious in advance that even where there is no sign of Chechen involvement, there should be, because everybody knows all Chechens are criminals of one sort or another. They are a nation of brigands.

One is reluctant to mention our mass media, especially television and especially after the *Duma* elections; our budding parliamentarians have proved no better. Quite apart from the ravings of a General Makashov, whose symptoms of mental deterioration are manifest even to a casual observer, if we turn to the so-called Russian National Union (ROS) led by Baburin, we find it raising the subject of 'the forcible repatriation of

citizens illegally present on the territory of Russia, also the introduction
of a visa regime for citizens of Central Asia and Trans-Caucasia, with the
exception of ethnic Russians' in its election manifesto.

This needs deciphering: all refugees, or simply people who have
migrated to Russia, all those Uzbeks, Turkmens and Georgians, and
anybody else who is 'not one of us'('us' being the ethnic Russians)
should be forcibly sent as far away as possible, say to Kolyma. Have we
really forgotten how such deportations ended in the past for those same
Chechens, of whom 250,000 out of half a million perished in exile? And
let us not forget the massacre at Khaibakh, where 700 people whom the
authorities hadn't been able to deport were burned alive in a farmyard,
including centenarians and babes in arms. The ROS manifesto lays out
what should be done with what they call 'insubordinate' republics:
'They should be declared to be in revolt and extraordinary measures
taken.' What kind of extraordinary measures? Look at what is going on
in Chechnya. The ROS is not in power, but manifestos of this kind are
current and have their ideological defenders. Incidentally, this was
published in the press and read by the general public. Is it a call to
genocide? Indubitably. There was no word of protest. Nobody now
remembers that in the far-off nineteenth century, under the reviled rule
of the tsars, when a Caucasian war was waged over many years and gave
rise to innumerable grudges and prejudices on both sides, nobody used
this pejorative, illiterate formulation taken from a policeman's report,
'persons of Caucasian nationality', which was soon followed by 'persons
of Tatar nationality', 'persons of Cuban nationality', and so on. In the
past there were no 'gooks' or '*dukhs*'. Our enemies were respectfully
enough called 'hillmen', while those fighting on our side against them
were 'the Caucasians'. Travelling through remote Chechen settlements, I
heard many tales of how, flung into exile in the snows of Siberia and
Kazakhstan by that 'best friend of all the peoples', Comrade Stalin, the
Chechens' lives were saved by Kazakhs and Russians who would take in
children who were perishing after the death of their parents. So what
terrible things have happened to us Russians since that we have become
so unfeeling and cruel? And worse people; much worse.

A few days ago, there was a fleeting mention somewhere that ten
years have passed since the incident in the Central Writers' Club in
Moscow when blackshirts from the *Pamyat* (Memory) Society ran amok
at a meeting of the liberal April group of writers. For the first (and

admittedly also the last) time, the leader of the bullyboys, a certain
Astashvili, was brought to court and sentenced to several years in prison
where he ended his days.

But Russia is a strange state. We are quite capable of locking a man
up for several years for stealing a sack of potatoes or a couple of
chickens. There are endless such cases coming before the Commission
for Clemency, of which I am a member. Meanwhile, major scoundrels
flourish openly and are even members of the *Duma*. The promotion of
racism and Nazism, on the other hand, attracts no opprobrium, as if it
didn't matter. We are already seeing on television great sturdy thugs with
swastika-like emblems on their sleeves vigorously raising their arms and
bawling 'Sieg Heil!', and in one of the largest cities in the south of
Russia an enormous hall applauds them tumultuously. In a time of crisis,
unemployment and uncertainty, they are seen as a strong force, capable
of defending Russia from her potential enemies; their ranks are growing
rapidly, their ideas finding adherents and their actions are becoming ever
more aggressive. For the time being their sphere of action is small, local
wars – Chechnya, Transdnestria and, more recently, Serbia. All they need
is to have the enemy, external or internal, identified for them; and to all
intents and purposes that has already been done: it is still the Jews, the
intellectuals, the liberals. Censorship, surreptitiously reintroduced during
the latest events in Chechnya, the hastily revived defence contributions
(*oboronka*) paid a couple of times a year and a patriotically minded
populace united in its support of an unjust war, all this is coming to pass
in new Russia as it greets the new millennium.

How very reminiscent it all is of the revival of Germany in the 1930s:
there the Reichstag was burned down by who knows whom, here
apartment blocks have been blown up by persons unknown ... and the
result is a general desire for a strong power capable of protecting us from
our fear of powerlessness. Ten years ago I was in Latvia when the Special
Squads of the Soviet Militia were terrorising the capital, Riga. The
Latvians were building barricades from concrete blocks around their
television studio and on the square beside the cathedral, and I was in
there with them, because I believed that freedom has no nationality. We
were fighting for the freedom of all of us. And then we were victorious,
and Latvia really did become free; and then I heard an ethnic Latvian
speak of Russians with ill-concealed hostility. Not all Russians; for the
time being, only those Russians who lived in Latvia and who, in his

words, had occupied and colonised his country and deprived it of its national character. Now the familiar ethnic cleansing seems to be taking place, passports, visas: 'Our people stay, the rest can get out.'

That little phrase was first heard among our soldiers in the Caucasus, and here it is now, being repeated in faraway, civilised Latvia. I heard it from the editor of a publication with which I had collaborated in drawing up and publishing my freedom-loving appeals to the people of Latvia. He was a changed man. I suppose he was saying what was politically expedient. It was evidently expedient for someone to shut down Adolf Schapiro's theatre, one of the republic's best Russian-language theatres. And even the Writers' Resort in Jurmala where I stayed, and where like, true internationalists, Estonians, Lithuanians, Swedes, and Russians lived together in harmony and shared their experience as writers, proved not really necessary, and indeed even not expeditious because of its links with suspect Moscow. We are in no hurry now to go back to Jurmala which we loved, but why are even our Latvian friends, writers who hesitate after gaining their long-awaited freedom to answer our telephone calls, so ill at ease? And when former Nazis are ostentatiously marching in uniform through the streets of Riga celebrating their anniversaries, I no longer know what I was standing up for then in Riga: whose freedom I was defending on the barricades. And was it worth paying for with the most valuable thing I possessed, my manuscripts which my fellow tenants destroyed on my writing desk in retaliation for my presence on the barricades?

Going back to those far-off years in the children's home, I can say unambiguously that for us children someone's nationality was of no importance whatsoever. There was a boy called Motya in the Tomilin home, he was cheerful and kind, got on with everybody and deferred to nobody. He was our unofficial leader, one of us, even though there were plenty of thugs and petty crooks with power over us. In one of my novellas I sketched Motya just as I remembered him, and an observant journalist friend said to me in amazement: 'Listen, this Motya of yours, was he a Jew?' I was taken aback by the question and had to think. 'Yes, I suppose he was. But I didn't think about that at the time. Why would it matter to us?' Thinking back to the children's homes, schools, boarding schools and settlements I passed through, I cannot remember a single instance of anti-Semitism or racism among the children, unless it came down from the young thugs, older than us, who found themselves a warm nest for the winter in the orphanages. They had a well-established hierarchy and we were in no doubt that we were the small fry. Any of the big *khitniks* could eat us for breakfast; and we knew that some day we would ourselves be the big fish, and then we in our turn would eat the small fry. This ideology came from the cruel criminal world, and like today's television it easily took root in our minds. But it was not human nature: it invaded from a different, hideous world that was to swallow up many of us.

I have never managed to contact the friends of my childhood again. I suspect they ended their days in prisons and camps. But that is not the point. Neither Nazism nor racism are present as original sin in children who are just beginning life; they are born internationalists one and all, just as the Almighty decreed. It is only later, within the family, at school, in the street, from peer groups, that prejudice begins to break through with its ability to subvert any primal truth, especially if it falls on fertile soil. And here nothing helps, neither education, nor your profession, nor even belonging to that profoundly respected elite, the so-called intelligentsia. We have, after all, in recent years witnessed an entire Union of Writers bonding creative people together around a platform which may have appeared to be national but was, in reality, nationalist. Its attacks on 'un-Russian' literature – I will refrain from naming great names – do not fit within any definition of civilised behaviour, unless we are to start burning books by writers who are not 'one of us'. The writer Yury Nagibin, who all his life bore the heavy burden of being a Jew, discovered by chance only at the end of his days that he was, in fact, ethnically Russian; at the end of one of his novels about anti-Semitism, he comments wryly that, while it is hard to be a Jew in Russia, it is even harder to be a Russian. The persecution of any minority stamps its persecutors with a particular moral stigma. An inferiority complex develops independently of the level of guilty involvement, but is more pronounced in those who have more of a conscience. As the poet Aroslav Smeliakov put it, 'For all that we achieved and for our transgressions, for all that truly were the acts of Rus, our generation, shunning intercession, consents to put its neck into the noose.' ❏

Anatolii Pristavkin is chair of the Russian Presidential Appeal Committee in Moscow. The Inseparable Twins *is published by Picador UK. Translated by Arch Tait*

RAFAL PANKOWSKI

Met any Jews lately?

Aided by an apathetic media and the indulgence of fellow politicians, the far right has entered the heart of Polish mainstream politics

Ethnic minorities in Poland are few; its Jewish community barely 10,000 strong. Yet anti-Semitism is the most common form of racism. Infants may not imbibe it at the breast, but they are certainly nourished on it later: by extreme nationalist propaganda in the press and on radio, by members of the clergy, teachers and marginal but militant chauvinist politicians. Not everyone gets obsessively xenophobic, of course, most people seem to be immune, but it's undeniable that virtually every Pole is bound to encounter anti-Semitism in some form, somewhere, even if he has never actually met a Jew.

Racism can be treated in two ways. It can be acknowledged as a real problem and opposed, or persistently denied along with the consequences. The UK chose the first approach after the publication of the Macpherson Report in February 1999. Polish politicians have adopted the second: denial and trivialisation. The government has an ally in a large sector of the mainstream media that seldom publish anything on racism, xenophobia and the violence they provoke. What does appear is, on the whole, pretty unprofessional.

In Germany, where public opinion is heavily sensitised to any form of anti-Semitism or right-wing extremism, things are different. The contrast between Polish and German attitudes is strikingly reflected in statements made by government representatives from both countries during last year's conference on the extreme right in Frankfurt-am-Oder. Fifty years after WWII, the conviction that fascism has no right ever to be reborn is a central tenet of German democratic culture. The Poles might be expected to be equally opposed to the political tendencies that cost the lives of six million of their fellow citizens. Not so: unlike their fellows in France or Belgium, Poland's extreme right had no opportunity to compromise itself by collaborating with the Nazis and did not, therefore, suffer the same post-war opprobrium.

Influential right-wing media like the magazines *Nasz Dziennik* or *Zycie* report any sign of right-wing extremism in Germany, Austria or Israel in detail. Similar events in Poland pass in media silence. Indeed, commentators in the leading newspapers react badly should anyone else dare to write on the subject – as though to write about racism were to expose a closely held family secret.

In November 1999, the apolitical, anti-fascist association *Nigdy Wiecej* (*Never Again*), published a shocking report documenting 19 deaths caused by racist or xenophobic violence in Poland over the last few years. A short note on the report found its way into just two national dailies: the centre-right *Rzeczpospolita* and the post-communist *Trybuna*. The remaining media, including the biggest newspaper in the country, the liberal *Gazeta Wyborcza*, preferred silence.

Meanwhile, racist political groupings are growing slowly but visibly. Their message is amplified and fed by national chauvinism. The most active are the National Rebirth of Poland and All-Polish Youth, both of which cater for young adults. There are also other groups of varying size with the word 'national' in their name and, over the past decade they have travelled from the margins of politics to the corridors of power. The next stage in the structural formation of the 'national right' – its infiltration of government – is under way.

In the early 1980s, the best-known leader of the extreme nationalists, Boleslaw Tejkowski, had the support of just a handful of pensioners and an only slightly bigger group of disruptive teenage skinheads. The group, which went under the odd and lengthy name of the Polish National Community-the Polish National Party, seemed a combination of Nazism and communism in caricature. Intriguingly, in the 1950s and 60s Tejkowski had been active in a very different ideological and intellectual environment. As a sociologist he was known as an opposition activist with revisionist views who worked closely with the legendary dissidents Jacek Kuron and Karol Modzelewski. He switched sides in 1968 and joined the regime's anti-Zionist crusade, acting as a witness for the prosecution in the trials of his former friends. As communism fell, Tejkowski made a bid to become leader of the Polish Nationalists. But his remark that the Pope and the bishops were all Jewish, along with his calls for a return to Slavic pagan cults, left him on the political fringe, in altercation with rival leaders of the revived 'national movement'.

But the seed was sown. Tejkowski and his party are still marking time on the periphery, but the younger generation of nationalists has avoided the same mistake and chosen to break into more serious politics. They have been remarkably successful. In 1995, National Democratic Party leader Boguslaw Kowalski became press spokesman for President Lech Walesa, a past master of political manoeuvre who flirted with all kinds of political groupings.

But in the long term, the less spectacular achievement of another group of fanatical nationalists, the National Right, has proved more important. In 1996, they joined the Patriotic Camp, a coalition of several centre-right parties, and subsequently allied themselves with the Confederation of Independent Poland, the oldest anti-communist right-wing grouping in the country. Finally, they joined the ranks of a broad alliance seeking to dislodge the post-communists who had come back to power in 1993. The alliance, Solidarity Election Action (AWS), embraced a wide range of political sentiments: liberal, anti-communist, Christian Democrat and conservative. It now governs the country.

Alongside the AWS, activists from the National Right (PN) are also in power. They succeeded in something their idol, Jean-Marie Le Pen, never quite achieved: a coalition and entry into government on the back of the conservative right. The PN leader, Krzysztof Kawecki, wrote his PhD thesis on 'The socio-political thought and action of the National Radical Camp' (a radically anti-Semitic pre-WWII organisation). Although he failed to get into parliament as an AWS candidate, soon after the elections he was appointed cabinet secretary and chief adviser to the minister of education. Another AWS candidate recommended by the National Right, Marek Biernacki, was elected to parliament before he could complete his doctorate on the political thought of Roman Dmowski (the historical ideologue behind Polish anti-Semitism). Today he is minister of internal affairs. Yet another politician associated with the PN, Marcin Libicki, is head of the Polish delegation to the parliamentary assembly of the Council of Europe.

The French National Front leader has often been acknowledged by

PN politicians as their model. They have published a Polish translation of Le Pen's *Hope*. They have participated regularly at the 'Feast of St Joan of Arc' celebrated annually on 1 May by Le Pen's followers in Paris. But the PN owes its position less to its international contacts (which include far more extreme groups) than to public enthusiasm for anti-communism and a brutalisation of the language of politics.

After the election of post-communist Aleksander Kwasniewski to the presidency, the PN held a demonstration in memory of Eligiusz Niewiadomski, the far-right fanatic who, in 1922, murdered the first president of independent, post-partition Poland because he regarded him as a Jewish-Masonic puppet. Supporters were encouraged to join the rally by means of a poster bearing the slogan 'Stolzman out!' and displaying Kwasniewski with a revolver at his head. According to anti-Semites, Stolzman was Kwasniewski's 'real' surname. Later on, Marcin Libicki defended Niewiadomski's motives in a parliamentary statement.

Not long ago, Libicki criticised a report on extremism presented to the Council of Europe in Strasbourg, claiming that in Poland there was no such thing. He was supported by the remaining members of the Polish delegation, including representatives of the centre and the left.

The presence of 'national' activists in government has had a predictable influence on the politics of the country. The ministry of education has been recommending the use in schools of a history textbook by Mieczyslaw Szczesniak that is widely recognised as anti-Semitic. The ministry of internal affairs has initiated a campaign, code-named 'Alien', intended to hunt out foreigners whose papers are not in order. The police have been mobilised to seek out people from Vietnam and the former Soviet Union engaged in the black market. A hysterical media campaign is presenting migrants as the main cause of crime in the country, although statistically their contribution is negligible.

In December 1999, pressure from nationalist and Catholic activists led by All-Polish Youth contributed to a drastic tightening of laws against pornography. The nationalist urge to censor has also made itself felt in Gdynia where an AWS councillor linked with the PN initiated a campaign for the withdrawal of local council funds for a theatre that dared to stage the old hippy musical *Hair*. In Bialystok, a town in north-eastern Poland, nationalists are trying to put pressure on the ministry of culture to withdraw funding from the Belarusian minority's magazine *Czasopis*, because of its supposedly anti-Polish publications.

Over the past decade, the far right has extended its power base and moved into the cultural arena where it can reach not only the older generation but the young. This makes the task of eliminating racism in Poland considerably more daunting. Right-wing culture has many platforms, from the sports stadium to the university. It incorporates the National Rock Scene promoted by mass-market right-wing weeklies, with records, concerts and T-shirts. It includes the music and anti-Semitic poetry of Leszek Czajkowski, the bard of the new Polish far right, and the xenophobic *Radio Maryja* which has hundreds of thousands of Catholic listeners daily. It embraces the press: from heavyweight quarterlies with titles like *Fronda* and *Arcana* (both funded by the state) to *Nasz Dziennik*, connected to *Radio Maryja*. For several years, *Fronda* has had its own programme on Channel 1 of public television. The choice of available reading is impressive: history, politics, philosophy and literary criticism are being given a far-right perspective. Even 'literary' works have appeared. Historical revisionism is flourishing and incorporates the denial of the Holocaust, which is officially forbidden. This first appeared in the form of Polish translations of David Irving, currently issued by the Ministry of Defence publishing house Bellona. In 1999, Dariusz Ratajczak, a research historian at the University of Opole, published a monograph questioning the existence of the gas chambers in the Auschwitz concentration camp. Opole is less than 150km from Auschwitz.

So are all Poles racists? Are chauvinism and xenophobia inextricably embedded in contemporary Polish political discourse? Not in the least. If the National Right and other similar groups sheltering under the AWS umbrella tried to stand for election on their own, they would doubtless be ignominiously defeated. Most people have probably never even heard of the National Right.

The presence of the far-right in mainstream politics does not emerge from the fact that it has significant public support, but from the frailty and superficiality of Polish democratic culture. Politicians tolerate colleagues who express racist views, the 'serious' media turn a blind eye, and the magic circle is closed. ❑

Rafal Pankowski is editor of Nigdy Wiecej (Never Again) *an anti-fascist magazine published in Warsaw.*
Translated by Irena Maryniak

GEORGE KONRAD

The pitfalls of community

Racism is a disease of the collective self, the expression of the boorish 'We'. The individual is weak alone and seeks support and consolation in the collective self. Joined to the robust community, the self-esteem grows

Communities are composed of many exchanged signs, some obvious, some not; the person who isn't familiar with the signs, the one who isn't 'like us', but a foreign visitor asking to be admitted, is made to understand that the locals do not consider him one of them.

It is difficult to gain admittance to stable, traditional communities, even harder to become at home in them; it requires the work of several generations. In Europe, one must be an immigrant of several generations to be genuinely at home where one is, but perhaps even that isn't enough.

What we are talking about is a kind of collective envy: you shouldn't get any of what I get, because I have a right to it (because I've inherited it, because I've worked for it) and you don't.

The state and all its wealth is collective private property. Those who have arrived recently shouldn't have a share in it, says one or another pure-blooded native. The permanent faces the moving, the immigrant, the one who hasn't worked for the patrimony of the state like the insider, the native and his ancestors.

The citizen who leans towards racism wants to share neither his individual private property nor his collective property. He wishes to set limits on immigration and quotas on how many outsiders will be allowed to acquire citizenship. The newcomer cannot live just anywhere, cannot study just anywhere, cannot get a job just anywhere.

The local is provoked, exposed to new habits and new hierarchies; the invader sometimes surpasses him, the native feels endangered, he doesn't understand the phenomenon – and all incomprehension is humiliation.

Anti-racism – the generous inclusion of others into 'we-feeling' and 'we-consciousness' – only becomes majority sentiment temporarily.

All collective consciousness (religious, national, class, etc) discriminates; discrimination is the fundamental gesture which seeks validation, or an excuse, say, in skin colour, or in a common characteristic of a group.

There are fluid overlaps between patriotism, nationalism, chauvinism, ethnicism, anti-Semitism and racism.

The identity of the enemy is not the determining factor, the essence is hatred of the other, the fellow man.

Cain is the racist; the farmer who hates the shepherd in Abel. This is like the ancient animosity between Hutu and Tutsi.

Love your neighbour as yourself? I do not love him, I hate him, says the racist, because he is the way he is, because he isn't like me, because he belongs to another group.

The local cannot hate and ill-treat his neighbour or whoever gets in his way in an *ad hoc* way; he must organise, validate and coordinate his own hatred with that of others, so he can sublimate it as proper, majority hatred sanctioned by public opinion. The individual has nothing personal against those he hurts or even kills. With the harm he does, he expresses his loyalty to his own group. Racism is ambiguous because it can appear to be love, positive enthusiasm for our own. It can be one of the ways for an individual to participate actively and loyally in society.

Killing is prohibited within the community, but it is allowed outside it, against the current enemy. Those who want to kill must come up with a reason, and racism is handy, even recommended. It enables them to depict the object of exclusion as a sub-human, monstrous, beast-like, mythologically evil creature.

War, and especially mass murder, needs the irrationally characterised enemy, in other words, racism. The people transported in cattle wagons can be slaughtered with impunity, like cattle, if they can be viewed as beef-cattle, non-people.

In the spring of 1999, the leaders and opinion makers of the most enlightened democracies acknowledged and ratified the destructive effect of NATO's Yugoslavian air strikes and the, at least, 500 civilian casualties (not to mention the deaths of young men who were drafted) did not give them moral qualms. This can only be explained by a blindness that puts the mask of the demonised Milosevic in front of the victims so we won't have to feel sorry about the people 'ours' killed.

This substitution is a relative of racism, since the assertion: 'The Serbs deserve it because they are bad' is no different from saying: 'The Albanians deserve it because they are bad' or 'The Chechens deserve it because they are bad' – black, say the Russians, though they certainly aren't that.

With the help of false analogies and mythological generalisations, political propaganda quickly arrives at the rationale of racism, always in defence of the most noble causes, of course.

The discourse of human rights has been gravely wounded. If it is permissible for one side to violate them, it is equally permissible for the other. If one can use the excuse of saving human lives to multiply the number of violent deaths through armed intervention – directly and indirectly – then that discourse loses its credibility, its validity and its power to restrain.

Why didn't the leaders of the West see that the air campaign would only exacerbate the existing problem, the number of casualties, the material catastrophe, mutual hatred and dread?

The main media easily quickly created an atmosphere in which one of the combatants appeared good and worthy of sympathy to the majority, while the other appeared evil and unworthy of sympathy.

Propaganda is a virus that makes the one who spreads it sick too.

If humanitarian rhetoric has lost its innocence because it has fallen into the sin of hypocrisy, regaining it will be difficult, perhaps impossible.

That is a serious problem: it opens the way for organised as well as spontaneous waves of xenophobia, for populism that uses the speech of hatred cunningly and within a democratic framework, for outspoken and righteous collective egoism, coded racism, withdrawals of empathy.

Once again: there are many branches of collective discrimination, hatred capable of even murder. Racism is one among them, by now it is hard to distinguish it from its siblings – radical nationalism, ethnicism, chauvinism, the other forms of collective scorn, hatred and rejection.

A significant minority of modern, democratic societies sees its main problem in the presence of another group of people, and devotes itself so completely to this passion that it becomes capable of instilling it into the majority. For the racist, the extinction of the hated group is synonymous with salvation. There are religions of love and religions of hate, it is not likely that either will disappear from the face of the earth and from people's hearts, they just remake themselves, find new targets, update their vocabularies and tool kits.

The racism capable of surprising us with its transformations likes barbed-wire fences, for example, because they are good for keeping people inside, but also useful for locking people out of what is ours, to the greater glory of the first-person plural.

Those who are against racism would do well to examine themselves first, to look to their own judgments and prejudices. ❏

George Konrad *was one of the leading figures in the Hungarian Democratic opposition before the transition of 1989, publishing in samizdat. Among his novels are* The Caseworker *(1969),* The City Builder *(1977),* The Loser *(1986),* A Feast in the Garden *(1985) and* Stone Clock *(1994 – to be published in English in the autumn of 2000).* The Invisible Voice, *his newest volume of essays, will be published in English this spring.*
Translated by Peter Reich

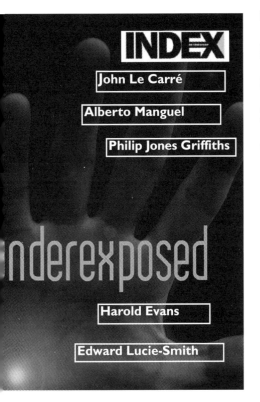

dog-You all hated him. Who? Damn! Who? ...Tell me. Tell me. Please tell me now. Who killed ...Who did it. You know who killed my dog? Do you know who killed my dog. I'll kill you if you know anyone killed my dog. How could anyone kill a dog? If you don't tell me now. killed my Dog. I missim. He was very much. Who did it? Who? Who killed him? Who are you-that you could kill a dog? Who killed him? My dog was the best.

Please was my best friend. I do... who did it? You do kn... you don't tell me who k... My dog was the best. Who killed my d... you could kill...

Culture

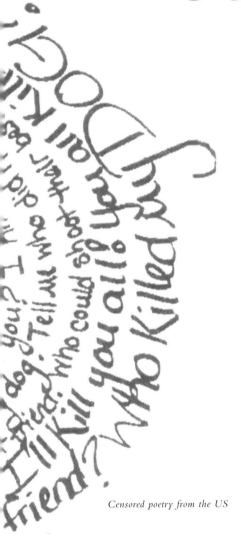

New fiction from Africa

Controversial photography from Birmingham, UK

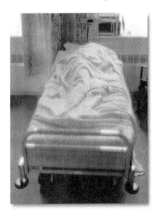

Censored poetry from the US

MICHAEL KELLY

Stories of an African schoolgirl

One evening, newly arrived in Burkina Faso where I was working with lecturers, teachers and students on an educational training project, I was leaving a colleague's garden when a girl I had never seen before greeted me. She accompanied me as I went on my cool of the evening walk. A schoolgirl: Dienobou Sanoussa.

A few days afterwards, she made her first visit to talk with me. Followed by many others. She quickly began to tell me about the difficulties, problems and unhappinesses of her life. 'Life is unbearable. Home, school, everything is horrible.' She told me about teachers' sexual abuse of schoolgirls, about the girls' defencelessness and their connivance. She talked about particular teachers and their behaviour, particular girls and their behaviour.

I asked if she ever thought of writing down these things. It was obvious her gift with words was outstanding.

'Writing,' she said. 'Writing is the only relief I have in this miserable life.' The next day she gave me her draft. The content is familiar, horrifyingly so, to all who have worked in education in West Africa. I was introduced to the subject in Ghana, in the early 1960s, at a *durbar* for teachers where the regional commissioner spoke of the unsavoury reputation they had for sexual exploitation of female pupils. As I was working in an all-boys boarding school away from town this was news to me. I asked Ghanaian colleagues about it. 'Yes,' they told me, 'such things are very common. It is known as "homework" because the girls who want extra tuition visit the teachers at their homes. Some of the teachers are very much to blame but at times the girls are at fault. They can enter the house, move straight to the bedroom, undress and lie on his bed and call the teacher. Afterwards, they may do some studying with him.'

The practice is common in other countries in which I have lived and worked: Cameroon, Nigeria, Sierra Leone, Senegal. But I have never previously come across a schoolgirl's account of such events and feelings. It is her originality and courage that I find so marvellous: she writes entirely freshly, a natural-born writer. I encouraged Dienobou to go on writing. She tells me writing relieves her rage and unhappiness, her disgust and shame. She cannot tell her father who is unapproachable; she cannot tell her mother whom she does not want to upset. She cannot afford to expose herself locally as responsible for such outspokenness, and disrespectful and scandalous lack of reserve. She offers them, therefore, to the eyes of strangers under a pseudonym. ❏

Michael Kelly *is an educational consultant who has worked in Africa since 1961*

DIENOBOU SANOUSSA

Circle of fire

'You've got "fail" as your mark in maths.'

'What? Are you joking?'

'Not at all. Look at the mark-sheet.'

'It's impossible. I did well in the test.' I showed my answers to my friend.

'You did well but the teacher has not given you good marks.'

'He must have made a mistake. With all the papers he has to correct…'

But he can't make mistakes of that kind. I'll have to take it up with him when we next have a class together.

So I showed the teacher my paper the next time he taught our maths class. He simply told me my 'Fail' mark was correct. He seemed to be bearing some ill-feeling against me. I racked my brains to find a reason. I came up with nothing.

I had decided that I would make sure I got the mark I had truly earned even though the teacher seemed determined to refuse to give it to me. In order to avoid making a scandalous scene, or provoking people to say that I was a girl who 'negotiated' her progress with teachers, I went back to my place in class. Nevertheless I compared my paper with others who had done better than I had. Their answers were the same as mine! I couldn't understand why this teacher was refusing to give me the correct mark.

During break I talked about it with my sister. She cleared up my ideas. My maths teacher had tried to interest me in having an affair with him a couple of days before the tests and I had not agreed.

'So that's the reason he's treating me unjustly! We'll see about that! I'll get my correct mark no matter what happens.'

I took my paper to the headmaster.

When I went into his office he said: 'What a pretty girl! Why do I have this honour, mademoiselle?'

I detest this flirtatious style but as I was the victim of an injustice I did not react.

'It's like this, headmaster … Please excuse me but I am going to speak directly. My maths teacher tried to interest me in having an affair with him and because I did not accept he has refused to give me the mark I achieved in the test he set the class. I have come to you so that you will correct matters.'

He listened to me, gently nodding his head.

When I had finished he told me: 'At three o'clock this afternoon… Come to see me at my house, mademoiselle. I am going to sort this out with your teacher. Just at this moment I am not free to attend to him. I have so many more serious things to concentrate on.'

That afternoon I went to the headmaster's house. He lived near the school so everybody knew his house, including me as I was one of his pupils.

He gave me a very comfortable chair to sit down in. He offered me something to drink but I did not accept, politely, because I had not meant to go there to drink.

'And my maths teacher?' I asked.

'He won't be long.'

I suspected that he might never be coming.

The headmaster seemed a bit ill at ease. I asked myself why. It was nothing to do with me.

After some moments he went out of the room into another one which I thought might be his bedroom. He called to me to join him: 'Come see what I have bought for the library.'

As I love reading I set aside my touch of disquiet over the room he had gone into, telling myself that I was wrong to be suspicious. Bah; perhaps it was his book room.

He did not wait for me to come through the door before he took hold of me and moved straight towards his bed. I resisted as well as I could, but I had forgotten that a man who is excited becomes as savage as a wounded wild beast.

I succeeded in getting out of his grasp and I cried out that he should let me go if the neighbours were not to learn what he was doing, so that I could talk with him about the matter that was troubling me so much.

'If you accept me, I can help you solve your problem,' he said, 'and see that you pass your test with high marks.'

'What do you take me for?' I said. 'For a sex-trader? I am not one of those.'

Point blank, he said to me, 'You are expelled.'

'Ah,' I said. 'Expelled. It allows me to decide how I am to behave.'

I looked for something really stinging to say, something really cutting that would hurt him, but I did not find anything. It was only when I got outside that I burst into tears.

The next day I was sent out of class, away from school. Reason: stubborn disrespect. I was not allowed back into the school.

It was at that moment that I felt we are attacked from all sides, at all levels. But even though that is the state of affairs, we can still break out of this cycle of fire. We must be aware. We must speak out. ❏

A crime

I never went stealthily to his compound without looking round to make sure that no-one was noticing me.

I knew his reputation with women and I felt an inner voice telling me not to go, but I tried my uttermost to repress that voice. I believed that, with me, things would be different; or that, for him, things would be different.

When I reached his house he wasn't there. I began to lose confidence. We had agreed to meet there at ten o'clock. Perhaps he had made this assignation on impulse; perhaps he had invited me because he thought I was a pushover. All these fears attacked me.

Twenty minutes later he arrived with all sorts of foodstuffs. This immediately resurrected him in my estimation. He apologised for being late and invited me into his house. I accepted willingly. We had a little drink together before we moved to the table to eat. The small change of getting to know each other. We chatted altogether informally. I found him full of charm, handsome. He didn't stop complimenting me on my clothes, on my beauty and I felt a sudden sense of coming to life.

When we had finished eating and clearing the table we moved

straight away to the bed. I no longer recall the details of what happened next. I only remember that at a certain moment I felt an acute pain. It was in that way that I sacrificed my virginity and it was for a man that I had always been waiting for. We have a proverb saying everything comes to those who wait. I told myself my wait had been rewarded.

When I left him I was bubbling over with joy. We were to see each other again the next day in the evening. I put on my smartest clothes; I put on a great deal of scent; I went to him. This time we did not bother with any delays because he told me he wanted me badly and he could not restrain his desire. It was the first time a man had talked to me like that. I felt I had become a real woman. It was not for me to be shy. I stood up and took him by the hand and led him to the bed and we made love.

Afterwards, we met whenever we could. He was a teacher and I was a pupil in the same school. That scarcely bothered me at all but it seemed to make him feel a bit awkward. He always seemed to be surrounded by a swarm of schoolgirls. Of course that made me jealous but I did not show it.

One day, when I went to see him, having become familiar with his house, I did not knock before going in. I made my way straight towards his room when I heard moans coming from it. I stopped, not feeling free to intrude. I did not know what to do. I thought it was best to sit down and wait because I told myself he would not be long before showing himself. As I was no expert in how people behaved sexually, I thought I should not jump to conclusions.

A few minutes later a girl came in, greeted me, and also sat down. No more than five minutes after that another girl came in and joined us. All this began to rouse my curiosity. But I took care to pretend no interest. I should say that I was not really worried. Seeing girls parading into the house of the man you love without any questions about where he was to be found was, all the same, a bit disquieting.

A moment later he came out, sweating copiously. The girl who had joined me first asked if he had found 'someone new?'. He said I was his latest conquest and that I had been well broken-in. I did not understand what he was saying. I asked him to explain to me. As if it was the most natural thing in the world he told me that all these girls I could see were his 'pillow-partners'; and I was his latest discovery.

He fell like a stroke of lightning in my esteem. Right to the bottom.

While I stared wide-eyed at him, the other girl said to me that I was well dressed. She could not afford clothes like that. She had to make do as best she could, come and rub up to him and purr, accept his terms: 'As he is a teacher he can give each of us a few francs at the end of the month. It's not much but it's better than nothing.'

'It's abominable,' I cried. 'It's sick! To give yourself to someone for 500 francs or less. You are not fruits in the market!' I had forgotten my part in all this performance.

I went out and made my way home. It was at that moment that I realised I was losing the being to whom I had most deeply given my trust. My eyes let fall the boundless hurt and misery I was feeling. I thought of committing suicide to put an end to it. But that was not a solution. I had to fight back. I had to show the world the outrages that are rampant in our schools, that destroy the confidence and self-esteem of so many girls. I had to show everyone what girls are subjected to in our 'educational' establishments. I had to put it all on record in black on white so that everyone would be aware. I had to cry out to the wide world to help us urgently.

Oh, you who read what I am writing, it is we, young girls at school, who need all the help you can give, our mothers, our fathers, our brothers. Dear female readers of my words, we must fight hand in hand for the cause of girls.

After I felt that I was going back to life, I found myself in agony. ❑

MICHAEL GRIFFIN

Positive negatives

The sense that one has been censored can become an obsession; and calling someone a censor opens divisions that never mend

Bill Morris's Jaguar Sovereign turns off the Soho Road and into the forecourt of Handsworth's City College, his *alma mater*. Bill's a big man in Birmingham and the most visible non-singing, non-sporting black celebrity in Britain who is not a newscaster. A child of the Windrush generation, the first wave of West Indian immigration to surf into Britain in the 1950s, he sidestepped the race trap and worked his way up the greasy pole of Labour politics to become general secretary of the Transport and General Workers Union – and a pillar of what is still a distant social hypothesis: an egalitarian, multiracial Britain for the twenty-first century.

Morris is a career model for Birmingham's 40,000–50,000-strong Afro-Caribbean minority, but his role tonight is far from ordinary. He is to make the keynote speech at the opening night of *We're From There: the Jamaican Brummies*, an exhibition of Afro-Caribbean life today by US documentary photographer, Larry Herman, a resident in the UK since quitting New York during the Vietnam war. An avowedly 'political' photographer, he has exhibited in London, Paris, Frankfurt and New York and is six years into a project documenting the lives of minority communities in Britain – the Bangladeshis of Bradford, the Chinese in Manchester, the Yemenis of Sheffield, Kurds in north London and Congolese in the capital's east. 'I go to communities that are organising in some form or another to build instruments to defend their own interests,' he explains. Over the last decade, Herman has garnered seven grants from British arts boards and sponsorship from Leica and Ilford. Now, passionately, he believes he's been censored.

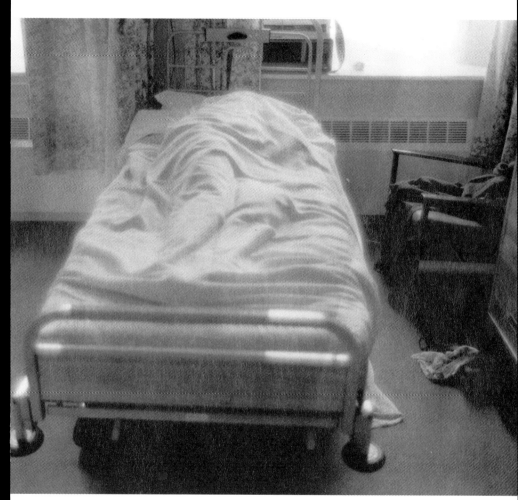

Young black man detained in the rehabilitation ward, All Saints Hospital, Birmingham – Credit: Larry Herman

The black-and-white images on the walls of City College proclaim
that, if he was threatened with censorship, it has not been successful. But
Herman's show was to have been mounted at Birmingham's more
prestigious Soho House Gallery the previous May, according to a letter
in his possession, until it was abruptly cancelled by the city council
following a disagreement over the way his images portrayed the local
Afro-Caribbean community.

'The decision was made on the basis that they "could not
satisfactorily resolve many of the major issues about the exhibition's
overall concept, tone and content",' explains Herman quoting from
another piece of correspondence. 'Now this is a subjective thing. On the
basis of my reputation and the quality of my work, they asked me to do
this exhibition and then, when they saw first-hand the type of work I
was doing and what I had to say about the community, they began to
retreat. I immediately rang people who were helping me within the
Jamaican community and their initial response was that "once again
whites are making decisions to speak on behalf of blacks".'

Herman worked on *Jamaican Brummies* for two years with the backing
of community leaders like Maxi Hayles, chairman of the Birmingham
Racial Attacks Monitoring Unit, who introduced him to different
organisations and individuals in Birmingham's black society. 'At first I
thought – and a lot of people think – that he must be somebody from
the CIA,' said Maxi, laughing. 'And I called a meeting, because I don't
want to take full responsibility for community initiatives. In the past, our
people have been let down by these researchers. You have everybody
coming to Birmingham to research black people and their reports are
just shelved. So we're guarded as to who we expose our community. But
somehow Larry, with this American accent, comes into town like a
whirlwind and we said: "Allright."'

When the offer of the Soho House show was withdrawn, City
College stepped into the breach, spending several thousand pounds on
what Herman portrays as an attempt to rescue his portrait of the people
from the clutches of the Birmingham art bureaucrats. There is little in
the images on display that suggests the photographer merited censorship,
even amid the relentlessly upbeat rhetoric that tends to dominate the
Town Hall's congress with its underperforming ethnic minorities. There
are cleaners, teachers, students, small entrepreneurs and car assembly
workers on the job, or in the pubs, churches and allotments that provide

their leisure. 'It's not a life of luxury,' said Maxi, 'but, at the other extreme, it's not a life of poverty either because we've made some good gains.' Though an exhausted loneliness permeates many of the scenes, only three have the potential to be controversial in civic eyes: one is of members of the Nation of Islam, another of a West Midlands police chief and a third of a shrouded figure on a hospital bed, a reference to local suspicions of racism at work in the National Health Service.

Herman's accusations of censorship understandably caused a ruckus in Birmingham's closely-knit photographic world, perhaps the largest since West Midlands police seized a book of Robert Mapplethorpe's erotica from the library of the University of Central England in 1998 (*Index* 6/1998). They have also been good for business because the censorship tag adds value and urgency to whatever product it is attached to, particularly when race is involved. In January, the exhibition was covered by the black newspaper *Voice* and the *Guardian* and Herman appeared on BBC Radio 4's *Woman's Hour*. The central topics raised were the censorship of Larry Herman and how a disadvantaged community had rallied round photographs which faithfully recounted their lives.

On the other side of town, a different story was being rehearsed by the black and white photographers who have made Birmingham a centre of excellence in the field of documentary photography over the past 20 years. They believe that the real victim in the case is the alleged high censor himself, Pete James.

Birmingham Central Library has one of the largest photographic archives in Europe, based around the bequest of a nineteenth-century photographer. As head of photography, James has spent 20 years trying to fashion that legacy into a collection that more closely reflects Birmingham's post-war ethnic mix by encouraging the work of such black photographers as Vanley Burke, Claudette Holmes, Pogus Caesar and Peter Max Kandhola, or by promoting projects like 'Handsworth Self-Portrait' (HSP). Conceived by Derek Bishton, Brian Homer and John Reardon in 1979, HSP confronted the issues of prejudice and power inherent in the relationship between the photographer, subject and viewer. Since the meaner streets of Handsworth in 1979 tended to condition the viewer's response to anyone trapped in the frame, Bishton, Homer and Reardon sought to eliminate the landscape altogether by erecting a closed, white canvas studio on Grove Lane. Passersby, singly or in groups, could drop in to have their photograph taken, collecting the results later in the week. In a further devolution of authorial power, the shutter release remained squarely in the subject's palm. Such issues remained crucial to fine-tuning ethnic photography projects long after Bishton and Reardon had moved on to successful careers in newspapers.

Pete James refuses to be drawn into making any public comment on Larry Herman's charges, which were, in any case, complicated by the fact that they had once been friends and collaborators. But Vanley Burke, who has amassed 70,000 images in some 25 years of documenting black life in Britain, is happy to defend the man who rescued his own archive after a fire and then raised £1,000 (US$1,600) for him to catalogue it. 'Pete has supported an enormous amount of people's work. People who would never have had the light of day put upon their pictures have been commissioned and produced work. So why should [Herman] feel it necessary to criticise this person? Why? Because his work is not deemed good enough … He's been refused a show and, as a result, he's playing the big child and is kicking up a lot of dust. And for that, I'll kick up dust.' Herman responds that Burke is prejudiced because he is 'dependent on Birmingham's money'.

'This is the first time,' Herman says, 'that, after a body of work has been produced, they've intervened and said they didn't like it, that it didn't accurately represent the community. Now they have no authority whatsoever to make those judgments. I was actually dealing with people in the community, taking direction from them: "Don't be afraid, Larry, photograph that!" This was the response I was getting from within the community and here are these people from outside the community saying that my work didn't accurately represent the community, when virtually everyone in the pictures had given their authority.'

'The first thing I ask when I go into a situation to photograph is "What do you want me to see?" I'll ask, "What's behind that closed door?" And, if they say, "Well, that's private", I'll say, "Okay". If they start to talk to me about it, after a while I'll say, "Will you take me on the other side of that door and let me see?" If they say, "Yes", fine. If they say, "No", fine. I'll find another door. But that also comes from my political view of the world. I am not a *paparazzo*. I don't hide in a bush, either metaphorically or in practice, because I ask people "What do you want me to see?" And I photograph it.'

But can it be a true version of the life of a community if you photograph only what they permit you to photograph?' I ask. Surely

that becomes a community self-portrait and no self-portrait contains all the warts?

'Well, that's true. Maybe I'm not interested in warts, maybe I am. Sometimes I am. Like the picture of Assistant Chief Constable Baggott. He's naked.'

'But there are warts on the Afro-Caribbean community as well. There's drugs, black-on-black violence, there's wife-beating'

'I have a photograph downstairs of a young girl holding a placard which says something like: "When you kill, you kill your brother".'

I suggest that's still a heroic photograph, a photograph that 'heroises' rather than a photograph of the actual truth, that looks tightly, closely at a problem in the host community.

We're interrupted because it's time to go and listen to Bill Morris. I'd asked Vanley whether there was any particular voodoo about whites taking pictures of blacks. 'Derek Bishton is white, John Reardon is white. They've produced a lot of photographs I wished I'd produced myself. I have no problem with that. As long as the work is done.' I put the same question to Maxi Hayles after the speech. 'So long as it's positive,' he answered, 'I don't see any reason against it. But it must be positive.' ❏

MG

ACLU

Squaring the circle

In January the American Civil Liberties Union took the case of 17-year-old Sarah Boman before a federal judge to overturn the expulsion of the Kansas high school senior for displaying artwork deemed 'threatening'. The ACLU asked the judge to allow Sarah's immediate return to school, but without the psychological examination required by the school board. The board had said that Boman must submit to a mental health examination after she wrote and displayed a poem deemed 'artistic terrorism'.

Boman's parents have said they would rather withdraw her from school than allow officials to subject her to unnecessary and intrusive testing. 'When will schools learn that different does not mean dangerous?' said Dick Kurtenbach, executive director of the ACLU of Kansas and Western Missouri. 'Punishing students like Sarah Boman only perpetuates the view that intolerance of difference is permissible.'

Boman's poem, written from the point of view of a madman who was angry because someone had killed his dog, caused consternation at Bluestem High School. The school principal expelled Boman for the remainder of the school year. In the wake of the Columbine High massacre, schools throughout the US have cracked down not only on violence, but on behaviour, dress, and now even writing thought to be aggressive, militaristic, or even unsettling. Boman said she created the artwork at the suggestion of an art professor at Bethany College, where she hopes to be accepted next autumn. ❏

More at www.aclu.org

BABEL

The silence of the damned

Up to one in four adults in Zimbabwe is HIV-positive. An estimated 1,500 people are dying each week from AIDS-related illnesses. Almost everyone has a relative who's died from AIDS. In spite of all this, silence reigns

*T*he hundreds of death announcements in the daily papers read only: *'untimely death after a short illness'. HIV and AIDS are associated with prostitution, so to admit infection is to bring shame on the family. The very word AIDS is so taboo that people avoid it, preferring to say, 'iyoyo' (that thing over there).*

In Uganda, where there is far greater public discussion of the subject and politicians have acknowledged that they are HIV-positive, the rate of infection has dropped sharply. Not so in Zimbabwe, where several cabinet ministers are thought to have died from the disease but none of whom has announced this publicly, not even posthumously.

The examples that follow are not in any way extreme or unusual. Women all over the country are censoring other female members of their families. But this is not a trait confined to women: Zimbabwean men are equally averse to openness when it comes to addressing HIV and AIDS. The difference is that men generally censor themselves by not declaring their status, whereas women are under family pressure to keep silent.

STEMBISO: I'm a mother of three children, and a widow. I live in Harare. My husband died in 1995 from AIDS. He started to be sick after attending his brother's funeral. The funeral was in an area which is known for witchcraft, so we thought he'd been bewitched. We travelled hundreds of kilometres and spent a lot of money seeking help from traditional healers, but nothing worked. He got weaker and weaker. I began to suspect my husband could be suffering from AIDS, but I was in a difficult position. In our culture the subject of AIDS is taboo, and I didn't know how to discuss it with my in-laws without offending them.

ERINA: I'm the first-born in our family of eight children. We were nine, but my sister Anna died from AIDS. She was 22 years old. I have three children. The youngest is HIV-positive. I wouldn't have thought it possible that I was HIV-positive, but then I got meningitis and I was in hospital for three months. I was very ill and they tested me. When I was dismissed from hospital I was still very sick so I went to my mother. My mother wouldn't accept I was HIV-positive. She accused me of pretending. She simply refused to believe me.

LIZA: I'm 24 years old. I have one son who's seven. My baby died last year. I discovered I was HIV-positive when my baby fell ill. I felt like killing myself. When people here discover you're HIV-positive they begin to reject you, especially relatives. They're frightened of catching the disease, so they stop talking to you. When my baby died, I didn't tell anyone it was HIV. Only me and my husband knew the truth, because I knew if I told anyone they'd reject me – just as they are doing.

STEMBISO: Eventually, a traditional healer told us to take my husband to a hospital. I got him admitted and asked for him to have an HIV test. He was mentally confused by now and I wanted a diagnosis. I wanted to know the truth, even if it was going to be painful. The doctor asked me if I'd desert my husband if the results came out positive. I told him I'd always stand by my husband. They took the test, he was discharged and I was told to return after six weeks to collect the results.
The problem came when I told my mother-in-law that I was going back to the hospital to collect my husband's test results. It was terrible. She told me not to go. She said his illness had nothing to do with AIDS and accused me of bewitching her son. She sent a family friend to get me to confess to giving my husband some traditional medicine to make him love me more. I told her I didn't do anything to him. My mother-in-law

didn't want to speak to me about it directly because she was worried I'd blame her.

LIZA: We had a normal funeral service for my baby. The people at the funeral didn't know she was HIV. But not long afterwards I got sick, and that's when they started saying, 'Your kid died of AIDS. That's why you're sick.' My husband told me to leave. He said he wasn't going to look after me, because I was the one who brought the disease into the house. But that's not true. I later heard that my husband had been married before, and that his wife and son had died. And he was unfaithful to me, bringing girlfriends back to the house. He gave me some money to travel to my mother's house, and I went. Since then, I haven't seen any sign of him.

STEMBISO: At one time, when my husband was still fit, he stayed out for the night. Zimbabwean men are very intolerant: if you accuse them of sleeping with someone else, they beat you up. So I was hoping my mother-in-law would help settle the matter. But she just covered up for him saying, 'Ah, he was just out with his friends. You are a jealous woman! Why do you want to stop my son having a good time with his friends?'

ERINA: My mother was very cruel. I was a bit like a person who was mad. The meningitis had left me confused and very weak. I wasn't able to stand up and walk alone. I would say, 'Mother, help me, I want to go to the toilet.' She would say to my sisters, 'No, leave her there, she can go alone. She knows where the toilet is, why should we help her?' I would struggle, shuffling slowly on my bottom. Sometimes, I would defecate before I got to the toilet. Then my mother and sisters would kick me and take water from the bowl and pour it over me.

LIZA: I collapsed when I arrived at my mother's house. An ambulance took me to hospital. When I was discharged, I returned to my mother, but she said, 'I don't want you to live with me. Go to your husband, he's the one who gave you this HIV! You must go and die with him.' I didn't know what to do, or where to go. Then a neighbour came and warned me that my mother had put rat poison in my *sadza* (maize porridge, the staple food in Zimbabwe).

ERINA: I tried to use a chamber pot but my sisters took it off me saying it was for children only. At mealtimes, they brought the food and put it down at the bedside. I wasn't strong enough to eat unaided, so I went hungry. I was very thin. My mother kept saying I was just pretending.

LIZA: At first I couldn't believe my mother would try to kill me. So I asked my grandmother what she thought. She tested the food on her dog. It died instantly. But I couldn't report the matter to the police because she was my mother. So I asked her about it and she said, 'Yes, I want you to die, you're troubling me with "that thing".' She said she'd kill me if I didn't go back to my husband. I didn't want to go back to my husband. He was very rough.

STEMBISO: On the day I was to collect the results, my mother-in-law and her family came into my room and told me not to go. They said I couldn't prevent him dying if it was AIDS, so there was no point in finding out. I told them I was going, whether they liked it or not. Then they asked, 'Who's going to look after your husband when you go to that hospital overnight? It's your duty. We're not going to do it.' It was horrible. I told them I'd nursed him for a whole year and they should manage for one night. Then they told me they wouldn't give me money for the bus fare to the hospital. I borrowed the money from my sister.

ERINA: Eventually my mother had to accept I was ill. She decided I'd been bewitched. She and my sisters were not touching my clothes or my blankets or my food. She wouldn't even sit near me and she told my sisters, 'Don't sit near her, because the illness will come to you also.' Then my mother said, 'You're a witch. I don't want you to stay at my house.'

STEMBISO: The results were like a big punch. My husband was HIV-positive. He was dying and there was nothing I could do. I thought I was going to die also. I'd lost a lot of weight. The idea came to me to kill myself, but then I thought: who is going to look after my children? I prayed to God to save my life. When I got back, I handed over the results to my mother-in-law. She called on her son and daughters and they all looked at the piece of paper. They told me not to tell anybody, not even my mother. She threatened me that if I told my family she would chase me out of their home.

LIZA: So I left my mother's house and came to this place where they look after people who are HIV-positive. I'm glad I have a place where I can live freely. Now I'm feeling I may live longer. If only I could find a place to stay with my kid. I don't think my mother will ever understand, because the 'sisters' who run this place went to her house and tried to counsel her, but she wouldn't listen. She said, 'I don't want to hear about "that thing". I just want to live in peace in my house.'

ERINA: An aunt told me about a place where they care for people with AIDS and HIV. Now I'm staying here. I was very sick when I first arrived. The people here went to my mother and counselled her. They told her a lot about AIDS. She accepts I'm HIV-positive, and she no longer thinks she'll catch it by sitting near me. I am learning new skills here, making mats and selling them.

STEMBISO: I decided to tell my family. We'd spent a lot of money on my husband, going to traditional healers trying to find a cure, and if I became ill, I didn't want my family to waste money in the same way. It was very difficult, because my mother didn't have information. She thought I would die that same year. Some of my cousins said, 'Why do you want to tell everyone? You mustn't do that.' But it was good that I talked, because I think it made me strong. I felt I had got rid of some of my stress. Other people, they keep it in their hearts and don't talk about it, and they get ill from the stress.
Two months after the death of my husband, I got a plot of land. And it was a great relief that I could go and live somewhere, just me and my kids.

ERINA: The difficulty is right now I don't have a proper place to stay with my children. I have a shack made of wood and tin, but the roof is leaking. My mother has taken my clothes and put them in her house for safe-keeping. So I know my mother can understand and cares for me, because she's saved my clothes from ruin.

STEMBISO: Now I'm building up my house, and I have a job as an AIDS counsellor. It really is a big problem getting people to talk about it here in Zimbabwe. It is such a great taboo. My job involves counselling AIDS orphans. Most of them don't even know their parents died of AIDS. It's difficult to help them when they don't know. Women should stand up and tell their children their father died of this disease, but they'd rather sweep it under the carpet, even if it means their children will die of the same thing.

ERINA: Right now I'm not well. I have TB again. But I don't worry any more about my health because I know if I die, my mother knows I'm HIV-positive and accepts it and she'll take over my children and will keep them.

LIZA: It's okay living here because all the people understand. It was a big relief to meet people who will talk to you about HIV. I wish some of my relatives would come and visit me. But they think if they even shake my hand they'll catch the disease. If I get to live outside again, I'll tell people I'm HIV so that they can see that even though you're HIV you can live long.

STEMBISO: I've recently told my 13-year-old daughter that her father died of AIDS. I think its really important for her to know, so that she doesn't go the same way and suffer like I have. I haven't yet found the courage to tell her that I'm HIV-positive. But I will, when we're both strong enough. ❏

Interviews by **Kim Normanton** *who is a freelance journalist, based in Harare*

All the women interviewed for this article are living or working at Mashambanzou Care Trust, a charity based in Harare

DANNY SCHECHTER

Old commies v dot.comies

Mega-mergers don't necessarily spell the end of diversity of opinion, merely the exhaustion of the 'old media' combines

The late Chairman Mao used to speak of 'antagonistic' and 'non-antagonistic' contradictions. The idea was that all phenomena have within them the seeds of their own destruction and that any analysis of political developments has to account for the unanticipated dynamics and underlying factors that scrape against each other like tectonic plates beneath the earth. Maoist thought may be in the dustbin of history these days, but this notion is not yet quite worth abandoning.

So it is with the new media order, driven seemingly everyday by new corporate configurations, mergers and conglomeration. The market logic that drives the media has sparked a branding war among the giants for what they call 'mind-share'. In the aftermath of the multibillion-dollar AOL/Time Warner merger, the *Wall Street Journal* spoke openly of their goal as 'domination'.

The implications are frightening, say a growing chorus of critics, including Mark Crispin Miller of New York University who runs the Project on Media Ownership. 'Now we have the prospect of AOL–Time Warner blitzing all of us, day in, day out, right where we live with endless, dazzling come-ons for other Time Warner properties. The whole thing, if I may speak bluntly, stinks: the anti-democratic deal rammed through by Congress and the White House; the hyper-commercialisation of the Internet; this particular monopolistic merger; and the other, similar mergers that gave rise to AOL–Time Warner.'

Culture and society are not all that is at risk: people's lives and livelihoods are at stake. Many of the employees of these merged monsters will be on the unemployment line. With the purchase of EMI by Warner Music, many heads will roll – much like the Seagram-Universal-Polygram deal a year ago. As former Canadian Prime Minister Brian Mulroney explained: 'I've yet to see a takeover that has created a single job – except for lawyers and accountants.'

Others have gone further and deeper in assessing the ways that large media combines will potentially choke off the diversity of perspective. It is true that the 'hyper-malling' of the Internet, in which users are customers first and citizens last, conflicts with the original vision of a decentralised new media open to all, uncensored by any. Even the talk about the Information Superhighway that once characterised White House boosterism has given way to acres of advertising for e-commerce of every description. In the music world, the ramifications of recent international mergers are chilling; four companies now dominate music distribution around the world.

Insurgent voices are being drowned out by the plethora of consumer choices. One sceptical British observer worries that 'the AOL deal – and the others that will follow – are sowing up the Net so tight that its "alternativity" is becoming marginalised. Filtering should take care of the rest. The Web is clearly mainstream commercial coalface now.'

But is it? I have always believed in pessimism of the intelligence and optimism of the will. Have we reached a Thatcherite 'There is no alternative', or are there options? Should we just allow the media beast to have its way with us? Have we gone from a fear of the commies to a subservience to the dot.comies?

So far, most of the money made on the Internet has been made on stock, not substance. Even Amazon.com, which pioneered a high-profile model of cyber-retailing, is in trouble. Reporting a US$500m dollar loss in the last quarter, Amazon rang alarm bells among investors who thought they had found an easy way to cash in on a high-volume business. According to a report by Morgan Stanley's high-tech guru, Barton Briggs, as reported in the magazine *Barrons*: since the personal computer came into use in the early 1980s, just five per cent of the technology-based Initial Public Offerings have created 86% of the wealth; the 241 major Internet stocks have a combined value of US$549bn, with sales of only US$24bn and combined losses of US$7bn.

True, this is still an emerging industry but, if these figures are to be believed, its potential has yet to be realised. Barton Briggs' take is that

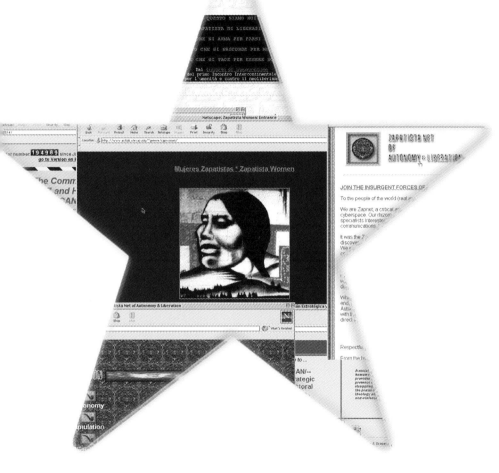

Zapatistas on the Web

the 'nature of technology is creative destruction'. Translation: this bubble is bound to burst.

Think of those 'Masters of the Universe', as an earlier generation of high-flying financiers were called until their wings were clipped and bodies jailed. Remind yourself of their rhetoric, their insistence on detailed business plans and skilled managers. Ask why they are falling for these dazzling online schemes and schemers? As one letter-writer put it: 'Give the markets some mystical technology, a few outrageous claims and venture-fuelled quick growth, then stand back and watch the feeding frenzy.'

Companies sometimes merge not because they are strong but because they are fundamentally weak. Time Warner was lugging around an enormous debt as well as a string of online failures that were embarrassing to recount. Each of their earlier initiatives had been hyped at the time of their well-publicised 'launches' and each had gone under, awash in red ink. Nor is AOL the powerhouse it pretends to be. It built its cash reserve and stock price on the strength of a monthly charge for e-mail and Internet connectivity. Now, as many competitors offer these services free, AOL could see the writing on the wall. The marriage with Time Warner was about distribution of its content.

All these companies are locked in highly competitive battles where some new unexpected technology can render them obsolete. Look at Microsoft, once the King on the Hill. It bet wrongly on the Internet, over-muscled its competitors and was declared a monopolist with consequences still to be made known. The computer revolution has its own graveyard of failed companies and investors who bet on the wrong chip.

Missing in much of this 'new media', of course, is what has been missing in the old media – a commitment to serving the public interest and elevating democratic discourse. While the Web still has many relative advantages in terms of its low entry costs, interactivity and potential as a global distribution platform, it is quickly being steered in a commercial direction and turned into a marketing tool. Does that mean there is no room at the cyber-inn for those of us who want something different?

Far from the big media view there has been an eruption of non-profit sites, with vast educational resources and a dazzling array of different perspectives. As a result, the Web is emerging as an organising medium, a way for activists of all stripes and on all continents to mobilise constituencies and galvanise political action.

One example is the Zapatistas in Mexico, a peasant movement that early on mastered one of our most advanced technologies. Another case is provided by the *Falun Gong* movement in China; it relies on the Web as a way to link and update its practitioners globally. It is no wonder that its use of e-mail and array of websites has driven the Chinese government to covert electronic warfare in an effort to disable its communications network.

While media companies merge at the top, there is synergising going on below that seeks to redress the power imbalance. Civil society is still much broader than corporate society. Activists and advocates who work together can build coalitions that get results. In the US in mid-January, the Federal Communications Commission announced plans to sanction thousands of new community-based low-power radio stations. This won't challenge the big media players, but they are nevertheless trying to squelch the move, claiming that their signals encounter interference as a result. This policy change is one small step towards democratising the media and allows ordinary people to be heard. It was won by a coalition of different interest groups with the Internet used as a mobilising tool.

With savvy marketing and clever branding, independent sites can still build sizeable audiences and challenge current trends. A significant number of opinion makers are turning against the media system. When that happens, more ordinary people will follow. We already have a crisis of confidence. In the US, viewer erosion is responsible for the lowest level of network watching since the advent of TV. Opinion polls report mounting dissatisfaction with media priorities. Sometimes it seems as if as many people want freedom from the media as freedom for it.

What this means is easy to recognise: the media system with all of its power is far from omnipotent and is vulnerable to still fiercer competition, increased calls for regulation and a dizzying pace of sudden paradigm shifts. And if Chairman Mao's dictum is accurate, today's non-antagonistic contradictions will soon turn into anatagonistic ones. ❏

Danny Schechter *is author of the forthcoming* News Dissector: Passions, Pieces and Polemics *(Electron Press, January 2000) and Executive Editor of the Media Channel (www.mediachannel.org)*

SALIL TRIPATHI

Soccer moms put in the boot

'Get into the car, guys,' Lisa Schneider shouts, as she hops into the front seat, wearing a yellow T-shirt and blue jeans on a bright, crisp morning in September, when the leaves take on incredible hues, transforming this part of New England into a painter's paradise. She starts the engine, and immediately a talk show surrounds the walls inside her Toyota station wagon.

In half an hour, Lisa will have driven from Greenwich, Connecticut, to Westport, and deposited the kids at their soccer club. Lisa is the so-called soccer mom, one of those thousands of women who voted Clinton and who will vote Bill Bradley or Al Gore this November. She is a liberal, half-Jewish, and hates George W Bush who, in her view, personifies all that can roll back the gains made by the women's movement in the US since *Griswold v Connecticut* and *Roe v Wade* (see p53).

Lisa is not just a soccer mom, she is also a supermom. In her spare time, she trades stocks on the Internet, listens to the Grateful Dead and can make the most amazing fajitas in Greenwich. Unlike the wives of some of her husband's colleagues, who spend their time at the gym, Lisa has put her degree from Amherst College to good use, and offers online tutoring to girls who want to write better essays, at US$100 a month per child.

So what's wrong with this picture of genteel, middle-class, suburban super-achieving existence, the kind John Cheever and Richard Ford bring to life in their stories?

Lisa uses NetNanny, a software programme that eliminates websites that are too pornographic, too dangerous and too anti-family for the discreet charms of this bourgeoisie. Sipping *latte* at a Starbucks coffee shop, she says: 'I mean, you know, I know that censorship is like wrong and all that, and I know that when I was a little girl I sneaked up to like my brother's bedroom to see if he was buying like reading *Playboy*? But things change when you grow older, and you want to protect your kids from stuff like that. You will do the same when you have kids.'

Three of her girlfriends, Anne Mifsud, Susan Everton and Liz Cornwell, nod their heads in agreement. 'Have you heard Howard Stern,' Anne volunteers. 'I mean, when my Martha is older she can decide for herself if she wants to listen to such shit but I must stop her from listening to it.'

They have railed against Internet pornography and bad rock lyrics in letters to newspapers and in Parent-Teacher Association (PTA) meetings. Lisa is for the First Amendment of the US Constitution that prevents the state from restricting freedom of speech or the press. It also allows the Nazi Party of America to march in Skokie, Illinois, in front of Jews, spouting racial hatred; lets Howard Stern make outrageous remarks on the radio; offers newsstand space to *Playboy*, *Penthouse* and their progeny; and lets Americans burn the Stars and Stripes or wave the Confederate flag, that symbol of slavery and racism in the eyes of many blacks.

And it empowers the press to a greater extent than anywhere else in the world. Only in America, for instance, would editors in the 1960s have published the *Pentagon Papers*, defying a president's use of the courts to prevent their publication. And in the 1970s, it was a US newspaper that began to explore a failed burglary that led, eventually, to the removal of Richard Nixon from the White House.

Lisa wants those freedoms. She says: 'Of course we need a vibrant press. But as a mother I have the right to control what my kids see and watch. I mean, they are kids, remember! They are 10, seven and five. At that age, they can't marry, they can't drive, they can't vote. So they can't watch unless I allow it.'

When Lisa stands up for her rights as a parent against the state, she belongs to the time-honoured tradition in the US that restricts federal power. But it has also led to piquant situations which allow a school board to decide what people in a community may read. It is a slippery slope.

Born in the US, Lisa has been raised with those fundamental rights that make up the US. But listen to Malini Desai, a US citizen born in Ahmedabad in western India, who moved to the US when she married her husband, Ajit Desai. Ajit works with a bank in New York state; Malini is with an insurance company.

Malini hasn't heard of the First Amendment; she grew up in India where 'reasonable restrictions' on freedom of speech are allowed. She wants such restrictions to go further. She would like to ban much that appears on late-night television: the Jerry Springer Show is out, Seinfeld, too. Even the popular sitcom Friends: all that kissing! And *Playboy*. And *Penthouse*. And, possibly, the Internet.

Malini says: 'We parents are working very hard. We have no time to cover what our children are doing. My husband comes home at 8pm. I come home at 7pm and I go straight to cook. You know, cooking Indian dinner takes time. I send the children to do their homework, but very many times I am finding they are watching cartoons on TV. Then I am thinking they were busy with homework on computer. And I find they go on Internet, and on Internet they can see anything. The last time I saw, they were seeing something really horrible,' and she looks down, too embarrassed to continue.

Malini has a point: for US police forces, paedophiles stalking children on the Internet relay chat is a growing problem, with some high-profile arrests, including that of a leading executive from a major software company. Some children have been lured to meet adults in public parks, and sexually abused. That's a crime, and there are laws to deal with it. But concerned mothers like Lisa and Malini want new regulations on the Internet and other forms of expression in the interests of their children that would restrict free speech for all.

To be sure, there have been regular attacks on free speech in the USA. School boards, often peopled by conservative, pro-family Republicans, who wear pinstripe suits and are church-going Rotarians, have kept authors like Kurt Vonnegut, Anthony Burgess, JD Salinger and Truman Capote safely away from the reach of schoolchildren. Many stores, including those of the biggest chain, Wal-Mart, do not stock certain CDs if they are deemed offensive to families.

This spans the conservative-liberal divide. Some books that deny or question the Holocaust are often taken off the shelf; the most recent author to suffer is JK Rowling for her Harry Potter series. Witchcraft, wizardry and adolescent adventures, according to some watchdogs, represent devil-worship, according to one such group. The conservative right taking on Harry Potter might seem laughable, but many such groups have significant power at the local and county levels and, in the prevailing climate of appeasement, some groups like Phyllis Schlafley's Eagle Forum acquire disproportionate importance. Once they were dismissed as fringe groups; not any more.

Part of the backlash is understandable. For all its pornographic television channels, triple-X-rated movie theatres and the violence in the media, the US remains, at heart, a country built by puritanical immigrants. Many Americans gawk when they see Europeans disrobe and strut around topless in the summer. Many more blush like teenagers when they walk through streets in Amsterdam and Stockholm.

Americans will never scrap the First Amendment altogether, but the separation of powers between the federal and local governments allows local groups to make strident remarks. And reasonable people like Lisa find allies in people like Malini and others from the Christian right. For the first generation of the new immigrants, for instance, the aim is to prosper financially while retaining the purity of the culture that they represent. The seductive appeal of the US mass media, which has made this vast country so tantalisingly attractive to people like Malini and Ajit, is also dangerous. They want the dollars, not the dildos. Their immediate response is to shut the windows and draw the curtains and rebuild a little Ahmedabad within those four walls to protect the kids.

It is an understandable, human tendency: the need to nurture, the need to protect. But even reasonable arguments tend to chip away at freedoms taken for granted. Mothers do know what's best for their children. But they may not know what's best for the nation; nobody really does. They have to accept accept that their writ runs only as far as their families: what's bad for Kyle, Chloe and Jamie needn't be bad for the majority of adult Americans. That's the American way. ❏

Salil Tripathi *is a regular contributor to* Index. *He is a writer based in London*

TheArtOfBarbie

The Art of Barbie exhibition will be at
Proud Galleries 3rd March – 2nd April
10 – 6.30 7 days a week

Proud Galleries
5 Buckingham Street
London, wc2n 6bp
Tel: 0171 8394942
Fax: 0171 8394947
E-mail: alex@proud.demon.co.uk
Wedsite: lastminute.com/proud

The Art of Barbie
Features over 40 shots of everybody's favorite doll,
interpreted by the worlds top designers, photographers,
artists and sculptors. All of Mattel's licensing royalties
made from the sale of this commemorative book will
benifit the Elton John AIDS Foundation

The Art of Barbie book is available from all good
book shops priced £25 published by Vision On.

support for

If you would like more information about Index on Censorship or would like to
support our work, please contact Hugo Grieve, Fundraising Manager, on
(44) 171 278 2313 or e-mail hugo@indexoncensorship.org

NEIL SAMMONDS

An image of flowers

On 6 September 1999 a dozen volunteers and the MP George Galloway set off from London on a red double-decker bound for Baghdad. Galloway is senior vice-chairman of Labour's Foreign Affairs Committee and co-founder of the Emergency Committee on Iraq, which campaigns against sanctions and war on the people of Iraq. In 1998 it organised leukaemia treatment in Glasgow for the five-year-old Iraqi girl Mariam Hamza, after whom the bus trip, the Mariam Appeal, was named. The group hoped to raise awareness of the consequences of sanctions, to demonstrate to Washington and London that the Arab world opposes the policy, and to show solidarity with Iraqi people

We had no inkling how we would be received on arrival at the Libyan frontier. 'What's this?' said the guard, pointing to the bus. 'A holiday?' I told him we'd come from London to campaign against the UN sanctions against Iraq. He looked at me as if I were a Martian. 'You're on holiday?' he insisted.

An officer bustled in to say there was a reception. Representatives from the *sha'biye* (popular committees) and the media welcomed us warmly in Ras Agdir, as they did at every town, whatever time of night we arrived. At one such – where we had been awaited 'with pleasure and desire' – sitting on the floor of a Bedouin tent, I was asked to make a short speech to camera. A dignitary leant forward and whispered: 'Try to mention the Colonel.' Everyone clapped whenever the words 'Brother Leader Mu'ammar Qaddafi' were uttered, a habit we tried to emulate for 'George Galloway', but soon dropped due to the giggles.

Crossing the Sinai desert – Credit: Neil Sammonds

The Libyan media covers Qaddafi relatively little, in fact. TV programming is impressive, with good documentaries on Libya's ethnic groups and social issues such as slavery. But there is no independent press. 'Any claim that a newspaper represents public opinion is groundless because it actually expresses the viewpoint of that private individual,' states the Green Book of Qaddafi. 'Properly functioning participatory democracy is the only real democracy,' a taxi driver told me enigmatically, wheeling past Tripoli's port. 'Now we have 30 ships in and British Airways and Lufthansa have regular flights again. We really suffered under sanctions.'

Four hours into the paperwork at the Egyptian border, four men storm into the courtyard. Representatives of the national campaign to lift sanctions, they have spent the day travelling to meet us. There is to be a

big public meeting tonight in Alexandria and we have to send a party
ahead. 'If the police ask where you're going,' says one, 'tell them Cairo.
They don't know about the meeting.' On cue, a Phil Silvers lookalike in
white uniform and droopy moustache approaches the border officials,
who point towards us. He strides up with his band of young colleagues,
makes as if to give me a handslap then tweaks my right nipple. 'How are
you?' he bellows. 'Are you 100%? Or like a government-market
chicken?' He roars with laughter and puts an arm round me. 'So now
you want to see the beautiful girls of Cairo,' he says, winking to his men.
Hamdi helps through the final hour of red tape. He's worked 11 years at
this desert post. 'Every day is the same, every day.'

The four activists urge us to 'go very, very fast'. 'We must lose the
police!' Bilko follows with his posse. A small ambulance pulls alongside.
The activists say they are *mukhabaraat*, secret police. The activists race off,
followed by the bus and Bilko's Toyota, the ambulance trailing behind.
Off the Mediterranean coast there are tens of carriers and battleships, the
sky's abuzz with jets, helicopters – Bright Star, the world's largest
multinational military exercise with 70,000 paratroopers and marines
storming the beaches. Our 37-year-old Routemaster is a transport of
delight, a symbol of civil decency against a backdrop of military
extravagance.

We reached a fork. The activists took the road to Alexandria. Bilko
ordered his Toyota to overtake the activists, waving on his driver through
clouds of sand. The activists reversed back and raced off, and we
followed. Bilko flailed in the wasteland; the 'ambulance' was confused.
We'd shaken off the State, ha! We raced on to Alexandria where I used
to live. Where crowds were waiting. '*Hasta la victoria, siempre!*' shouted
Stuart, clenching his fist.

Near Alexandria, the mobile chirruped and George was on the line,
telling us to join him in Cairo. 'But there's a massive public meeting in
Alex,' Stuart told him, '*Al-Jezira*, Arab News Network, maybe CNN,
they'll all be there.' George was adamant: we had to go to his meeting.
We told the activists there was a change of plan. Three went on to
Alexandria but one, the burly Mohandes Mohsen, squeezed into the
jeep with us.

'What happens if you complain against sanctions in London?' he asks.
'Nothing. No one listens.'
'I've been in prison six times for this. The last time for a year. I never

saw my wife and children.'

Three hours later we arrive at the five-star Hotel Semiramis. George walks over, cigar in mouth, new black suit, lovely wife Amina on arm. 'I heard about your speeches in Libya, brother.' he says smiling. 'That's the second Order of Lenin you'll receive in Baghdad.'

'What about this important meeting?' I ask.

'They left. So a few of us are having a lovely Chinese meal here. Come and join us, brother.'

I introduce Mohsen to George. He says: 'Tell him we're very angry. We spend two days driving to the border and back to meet you. You refuse Alexandria with its powerful unions and instead you come to a Chinese restaurant in a five-star hotel. Is this your revolution?'

George puts his arm around Mohsen, pulls on the cigar. 'Sorry comrade. But as Lenin said, for decades nothing happens. Then in days, decades happen.'

Mohsen frowns, smiles, frowns, hugs us and walks out of the hotel.

The bus lolloped east to Nuweiba to sunbathe by the Red Sea and wait for the Jordan ferry. The *fellaheen* from Upper Egypt, the Cairo businessmen, teenagers, pilgrims to Mecca and the crew knew all about the sanctions and the daily bombing. They knew of the banned pencils, medicines and shrouds. 'They're killing women and children every day,' said one boy, 'shame on them.'

We see three western tourists and go to interview them.

'What do you think about the sanctions on Iraq?' I asked the two young women and a man.

'No idea, mate.' said the man. 'Didn't know they were still on.'

'Yes you do.' said one woman, sucking on a Cleopatra, 'it's that Qaddafi. He's evil. He blew up the World Trade Building in New York. They should keep sanctions on them till he dies.'

Two days later we head east to the Iraqi border. Will the Jordanian troops ask us to hand over our syringes, pencils, medicines and the wheelchair? Will US marines storm the bus, as George has warned? How many media will be there? Accompanied by two coaches of international delegates and a lorry with 300 boxes of medicine, we reach the first checkpoint, a stockade of white buildings in sparse desert. We collect passports and head to the next, George's words ringing in our ears: 'The US will need its marines to rip these medicines from the hands of my colleagues! In front of the world's press! Then they will be shamed!' This check is a simple visa-flashing formality. We pass into no-man's-land. Even the medicine lorry isn't checked. Breaking sanctions is easy. No media.

I am in a friend's lounge in Baghdad watching the news. 'Saddam Hussein receives President Bouteflika of Algeria ... The Trade Fair is the largest since the 'Mother of Battles'... Israeli jets bomb South Lebanon ... US and UK bombers strike southern Iraq.' An image of flowers appears, signalling an item on Saddam Hussein, sitting stone-faced at a long table flanked by sheikhs. The first rises to praise the president, who places his hand across his chest at the end of the eulogy. One by one the others follow for a span of 45 minutes. Saddam finally speaks: 'From far, people have a false picture of Iraq. The real picture is of everybody in their suitable place.' The sheikhs clap, the programme ends, the flowers appear. A music show begins; Rick Astley sings 'Never gonna give you up'.

George is on the screen with his wife, Amina. They go to greet a besuited Uday Hussein. He smiles and dusts off his jacket with jewel-encrusted fingers. George relates a touching experience from Algeria: 'At the end of a massive meeting, a woman approached me and handed me her wedding ring for the children of Iraq. I told her it was too precious, I couldn't take it. Five minutes later she came back with her husband, who insisted on giving the ring.' This was the story. George then added: '"How can we be wearing jewellery," she said, "when the Iraqi children are dying?"'

Uday's hand was now conspicuously in his pocket. ❑

NS